THE GROWTH
OF CHURCH INSTITUTIONS.

# THE GROWTH OF CHURCH INSTITUTIONS.

BY THE REV
## EDWIN HATCH, M.A., D.D.,
READER IN ECCLESIASTICAL HISTORY IN THE UNIVERSITY OF OXFORD.

PUBLISHERS
*Eugene, Oregon*

Wipf and Stock Publishers
199 West 8th Avenue, Suite 3
Eugene, Oregon 97401

The Growth of Church Institutions
By Hatch, Edwin
ISBN: 1-59244-475-X
Publication date 1/15/2004
Previously published by Hodder & Stoughton, 1887

## PREFACE.

THE present work is an endeavour to give an answer to questions which are frequently asked in regard to the apparently wide differences between the primitive and the modern forms of some Christian institutions. It is designed less for scholars than for general readers who are interested in theological subjects. Its aim is to be not controversial, but historical. It is a summary of the results at which the writer has arrived from an independent study of original sources, and the meagreness with which some important subjects are treated is due to the fact that it is intended to be supplemented hereafter by a more elaborate work, which the writer has for some time had in preparation.

And since the work is thus designed for general readers, and is a summary of results rather than a detailed explanation of the facts upon which they are based, the writer has not thought it desirable to encumber the pages with more than the most necessary references to his authorities. But since the scantiness of the references may convey to some minds an erroneous impression that the evidence also is scanty, the writer thinks it proper to add that he is not aware of having made any statement which he is not also ready to support by sufficient proofs.

The work has the secondary aim of endeavouring to stimulate students who have leisure for historical study to give more attention than hitherto to the wide field which lies before them in the ecclesiastical history of the centuries which lie between the fall of the Roman Empire and the political settlement of mediæval Europe.

OXFORD, *March 16th*, 1887.

# CONTENTS.

## CHAPTER I.

### INTRODUCTORY.

The justification of the fact that Christian institutions have not always been what they are now is to be found in the nature of Christianity. The justification of the particular changes is to be found in Church history.

The present work is designed to show in outline the historical circumstances under which some of the more prominent institutions of modern Christianity came to exist, and which form the justification of their existence . . . . pp. 1—8

### THE DIOCESE.

What is the origin of the modern diocese? How was it that the majority of Christian Churches in the West came to have an incomplete organization?

The answer is to be found in the circumstances of the original Christian communities of Gaul and Spain. They were Roman, and not native, and in the cities rather than in the country. The Teutonic conquest at first both preserved and accentuated this state of things. The organization of the Church preserved that of the empire; the Romans who remained were viii *CONTENTS.*

reluctant to break through the lines of that organization by multiplying bishoprics ; and the power and prestige of the bishops, which increased as the old Roman party found in them a political as well as an ecclesiastical centre, came in time to render such a multiplication of bishoprics impossible. pp. 9—15

In Germany and England the bishops were at first missionary bishops, and Gaul and Spain furnished the model upon which organization proceeded when the missionary character of the Churches had passed away[1] . . . . pp. 15, 16

## CHAPTER II.

### THE DIOCESAN BISHOP.

How was it that the officers of one community came to have jurisdiction over those of another?

The common answer that presbyters were detached from the bishop's Church to take charge of outlying congregations covers only a small proportion of the facts. In the majority of cases in the West communities grew up independently of the bishop's Church, and their officers were appointed by the owners of the church-buildings. The danger to both faith and morals which this system caused led to a reformation, which was the result of the joint action of Church and State. Two principles which had long been recognised in the East, but which had been commonly disregarded in the West, were finally established :

1. That all the clergy within the *gau*, or county, should be subordinate to the bishop of the county town.

2. That all the bishops within what had been a Roman province should be co-ordinated into a single body, with the bishop of the metropolis at their head . . pp. 17—32

The first of these points was secured by a double provision : (i.) that every year the clergy should report themselves to the bishop ; (ii.) that every year the bishop should make a circuit of his district for the purpose of (*a*) preaching, (*b*) confirming, and (*c*) exercising discipline, both ecclesiastical and civil pp. 32—39

## CHAPTER III.

#### THE FIXED TENURE OF THE PARISH PRIEST.

How was it that the officers of these detached and incompletely organized communities came to have a tenure of office which was not dependent on the goodwill of either the community, the owner of the building, or the bishop?

It came, in the first place, from the necessity of checking, in the interests of the Church at large, the nomination and dismissal of clerks by the owners of churches. The endeavour to institute such a check was not in the first instance successful. The rights of ownership were strongly asserted, and several centuries elapsed before they were finally set aside    pp. 43—50

It came, in the second place, from the gradual recognition of the claim of detached Churches to enjoy their own revenues. The bishops were for a long time the only spiritual persons who could hold property as such. They held all the property and claimed all the revenues of all the Churches within their district. There were successive stages of compromise by which a bishop received (1) a third or fourth, instead of the whole, of the revenues of such Churches; (2) presents instead of a fixed proportion; (3) fixed fees instead of presents    .    pp. 51—56

## CHAPTER IV.

#### THE BENEFICE.

How was it that the ministers of detached Churches came to have not merely a fixed tenure, but also a freehold right?

The answer is to be found in a combined consideration of the modes in which gifts of land were made to the Church, of the enormous extent of such gifts, and of the prevalent systems of land tenure. The modes of gift were mainly three: (1) by unconditional donation in a man's life-time; (2) by will; (3) by donation with reservation of the usufruct. The extent of such gifts was so great as to give rise to many legal checks. But, in spite of checks, the bishops often became the chief land-x    *CONTENTS.*

owners in their dioceses. It became impossible for them to cultivate their lands themselves. Hence the system of leasing Church lands grew up, and was in some cases forced upon the Church by the State. Lands so leased were said to be held *ad beneficium* . . . . . . . pp. 61—72

Sometimes lands were leased in this way, not to laymen, but to the ministers of parish churches, as a source of income. 1. In some cases they were so leased by a bishop, a practice which exists in modern times, under the name of "collation." 2. In some cases they were so leased by a layman, a practice which underlies the modern system of patronage, with the important difference that the feudal rights of the original owner have passed to the bishop . . . . . pp. 73—77

## CHAPTER V.

### THE PARISH.

How was it that the local Church came to be regarded as standing in a special relation to the district which surrounded it? *i.e.*, How did the idea of a congregation pass into that of a parish?

The basis of the conception is probably pagan. The Christian superstructure is probably due to two causes, viz., (1) the regulations as to baptism, which required it to take place in certain designated churches; the inhabitants of a district were required to present their children for baptism in such churches, and a special relation thus came to exist between the district and the "baptismal" church. (2) The regulations as to the payment of tithes. At first a certain liberty of choice existed as to the church to which a man might pay his tithes; this liberty came gradually to be restricted; the tithes of every farm were assigned to a "baptismal" church in its neighbourhood .

pp. 82—89

The area of a baptismal church—*i.e.*, the original parish—was that of the modern "rural deanery;" the chief officer of such a church was an archpresbyter, or rural dean, who exercised over the clergy of the district powers similar to those of the officer who bore the same designation in the bishop's church. In course of time, as the population increased, these areas were found too large ; new churches were erected, and tithes were assigned to them ; and every such church came to have round it an area whose boundaries were, in fact, the boundaries of the farms from which they could claim tithes. The conception of the presbyter as an officer with spiritual control over a certain area ousted the conception of him as the minister of a congregation.

pp. 89—97

## CHAPTER VI.

### TITHES AND THEIR DISTRIBUTION.

Tithes are not an immemorial institution of the Christian Church. They practically date, as a Christian institution, from the eighth century. They were originally a rent paid for the lease, compulsory or otherwise, of Church lands. When they once came into use the amount of the rent so paid suggested an analogy with the Levitical tithe, and the analogy was strongly pressed. They tended to become a payment from all lands, whether leased or otherwise, and were in reality a customary measure of freewill offerings . . . . . . pp. 101—108

Tithes followed the rule of all offerings to the Church in being at first at the disposal of the bishop for all the needy persons on the Church list, and in being afterwards divided in certain fixed proportions. These proportions varied slightly, sometimes four parts being mentioned, and sometimes three ; but the poor and the clergy were always placed on the same footing in both ecclesiastical and civil enactments . .

pp. 108—117

## CHAPTER VII.

### THE METROPOLITAN.

The custom of holding periodical meetings of neighbouring bishops led to the systematizing of such conferences by requiring them

to be held, as similar civil meetings were held, on the lines of
the provinces of the Roman Empire, with the bishop of the
metropolis of the province as their president. The system
spread from the East to the West, but with the decay of the
Empire in the West it tended to fade away . . pp. 122—127

The revival of the system was due to Boniface, and the
development of it to Charles the Great. The metropolitans
became not only heads of the Church, but also great officers of
state. As such they pressed their personal authority. The
suffragan bishops were made to feel a subordination which
ultimately produced a reaction. The Roman see supported
the bishops against the metropolitans, and the pseudo-Isidorian
decretals were the successful instrument by which bishops and
metropolitans alike were subordinated to Rome. Some powers
afterwards came back to metropolitans as papal delegates, and
these have to some extent remained, even when the check of the
Roman see has been withdrawn . . . pp. 128—135

## CHAPTER VIII.

### NATIONAL CHURCHES.

National Churches grew out of the same causes which had produced
provincial Churches. The grouping of Christian communities
according to the lines of Roman provinces passed into the
grouping of them on the more shifting lines of the newly
formed kingdoms of Western Europe. The assemblies which
took the place of the provincial assemblies were as much civil
as ecclesiastical, and out of them came the idea of the nation
as constituting not only a political, but also an ecclesiastical unit
pp. 139—144

These points are shown (1) by the fact that the assemblies
were summoned by kings, and not by bishops ; (2) by the fact
that they consisted of both clergy and laity ; (3) by the fact that
their resolutions refer to spiritual and ecclesiastical as well as
to secular and civil subjects . . . . pp. 139—154

## CHAPTER IX.

### THE CANONICAL RULE.

Heathenism died hard, and the Christian clergy were for a long time degraded by contact with it. There is clear evidence that in the eighth century the level of morality and discipline was low. A reaction against current practices came from monasticism. Clergy-houses were established, and the majority of the clergy were compelled to live in them according to a common rule of life. The system ultimately became compulsory, and the rule of life was promulgated by the civil power. It aimed (1) at discipline; (2) at edification and instruction. The first of these was mainly enforced by the penitential system; out of the second grew many of the schools and universities of the middle ages . . . . . . pp. 157—172

## CHAPTER X.

### THE CATHEDRAL CHAPTER.

The clergy of a city, who then lived together in a common building and under a common rule, were in the first instance only the clergy of the bishop's church, living under the bishop's eye. In course of time those who thus lived together, though living near the bishop's church, ceased to live in the bishop's house, and came both to be independent and to have an internal organization of their own. 1. They came to be independent of the bishop, because they had a right to acquire and hold property: hence (*a*) they acquired a corporate character; (*b*) their numbers were limited; (*c*) the property was subdivided and assigned to individual clerks and their successors; (*d*) the membership of a clergy-house became a position of dignity and emolument, and the duties of the office came to be assigned to deputies. The result was a practical subversion of the purpose for which both clergy and clergy-houses existed  pp. 176—182

2. They came to have a separate internal organization, whence the modern dean, canons, and prebendaries .

pp. 183—190

## CHAPTER XI.

### THE CHAPTER AND THE DIOCESE.

The clergy of the bishop's house, who thus came to be independent of the bishop and to have an organization of their own, came also in course of time to absorb the functions of the whole body of the clergy of the diocese. The early distinction between the clergy of the bishop's city and those of the district over which the bishop had jurisdiction led to a distinction between the ordinary and the occasional council of the bishop. The former tended to take the place of the latter; and the ordinary administration of the diocese, which was theoretically in the hands of the bishop and the whole body of his clergy, fell first into the hands of the bishop and the clergy who immediately surrounded him, and at last into the hands of the bishop alone . . . . . . . . . pp. 193—200

The part of the original theory which survived longest was the election of bishops. There was for many centuries a struggle between Church and State, but where the Church was able to assert its own position the election of bishops was at first by the clergy and laity of the diocese, then by the clergy and laity of the city; it was only by slow degrees that the election by cathedral chapters became the common rule . pp. 200—208

## CHAPTER XII.

### THE CHANCEL.

The multiplication of clergy-houses tended to separate the clergy from the laity more than before. The separation expressed itself (1) in a more complete local separation in Divine worship; (2) in a separate dress.

1. The clergy of a church came to be more numerous and to require a larger space. This led to an increase in the size of the choir. And since they were required to attend services several times a day, while the rest of the church was comparatively

deserted, the place of the clergy came to be separated from that of the laity by a screen. The altar remained in its original place, and this being sometimes inconvenient for the clergy, another altar was placed in their own part of the church, and the communion of the clergy came to be distinct from that of the laity. Round the choir a passage was sometimes constructed, which had the effect of further isolating it . pp. 213—221

2. The clergy of a clergy-house came to be distinguished by a special dress. Monks wore a woollen dress, but clerks might wear linen and fur. In the winter their ordinary dress was a fur coat; over it in church a linen blouse was thrown, the later "surplice," which thus became the distinctive mark of one who, whether in holy orders or not, lived in a clergy-house . . . . . . . . pp. 221—223

The altered place of the bishops' seat in church, which, instead of being raised at the end of the apse, in a position of obvious presidency, came often to be at the end of one of the rows of canons' stalls, is a visible indication of the strength of the canonical system . . . . . pp. 223—225

*THE DIOCESE.*

# I.

## *THE DIOCESE.*

THE differences of outward form between primitive and modern Christianity have been a frequent theme of comment and of misconception. There are some persons who have endeavoured to base upon the existence of such differences an objection against Christianity itself. There are others who find it hard to reconcile them with their conception of the Church as a Divine institution. There have been, from time to time, large bodies of earnest men who, being unable to see a justification for this or that particular point of difference, have separated themselves from the main body of Christians, and formed separate communities, in order to restore, as they have thought in their own practice the uncorrupted simplicity of primitive usage.

The justification of the existence of differences is to be found in the nature of Christianity itself. It was designed to be at once universal and permanent, to embrace all races of mankind, and to meet the needs of successive ages. The presumption is that, this being so, it was also designed to adapt its outward forms to the inevitable changes of human society, and that its earliest institutions were meant to be modified when it gathered new races of men into its fold, and came into close contact with new elements of human life. The presumption does not run counter to any words, or to any clear inference from any words, of the New Testament, and it has been universally accepted by all Christian communities. For however much Christian communities have differed among themselves as to the legitimacy or expediency of this or that particular change, they have all accepted the fact and the necessity of change, and have all diverged in greater or less degree from the forms and practices of primitive times.

The justification of particular differences, and the justification also of those who adhere to the main body of Christians in spite of such differences, is to be found in the course of Christian history. The differences are great when an ancient is put side by side with a modern form. But between the ancient and the modern form lies a long series of changes, which are linked together by the strong bond of historical continuity, and which pass into one another by an almost imperceptible transition. Each link in the series carries with it its own justification, if it is found to be a natural and inevitable result of historical circumstances, a modification of an institution or a usage which was forced upon a community by the needs of a particular time. It is true that a change which has once established itself has not gained by the fact of such establishment a right to perpetuity; but on the other hand it does not follow that such a modification of a Christian institution should be abolished as soon as the historical circumstances which gave rise to it have passed away. We cannot, without risk of enormous loss, and only under the rarest circumstances, cut the moorings which bind us to the past. The ecclesiastical institutions which have come down to us are, even more than the political institutions, a sacred inheritance which we may legitimately endeavour to improve, but which we cannot lightly abandon.

It is proposed in the present pages to take some of the more prominent institutions of modern Christianity, and to trace the historical circumstances under the pressure of which their ancient forms were gradually modified until they came to be in effect what they are now. It will be necessary, for this purpose, to deal mainly with a period of history which has been frequently neglected, and which having been neglected has been commonly misunderstood. It will be necessary, also, to deal less with our own country than with the continent of Europe, from which, chiefly under the influence of the Roman see, many forms of our ecclesiastical institutions were derived. It will be found that the study of this transition period on the continent of Europe, by the aid of the large mass of documents which remain, will enable us to account for almost all that is distinctive in modern as compared with primitive Christianity. We shall be able to see by what gradual steps the congregational system of early times passed into the diocesan system of later times (Chapters I. and II.) ; how it came about that when the officers of some communities had become subordinate to the officers of other communities, they yet attained a virtual independence in respect of fixity both of tenure and of income (Chapters III. and IV.) ; how these incompletely organised and subordinate communities came, no less than the bishops' churches, to have a local area of jurisdiction ; and how the growth of the practice of paying tithes added whatever elements might have been wanting to their establishment as new units of organisation (Chapters V. and VI.) ; how the communities came to be grouped together in larger combinations on the political lines, first of the Roman administration, and afterwards of the newly-formed kingdoms of the West, so as to form the important aggregates, or units, which are known as national Churches (Chapters VII. and VIII.) ; how the reaction against the decay of morals, and the revival of monasticism, led to the successful endeavour to create for the clergy a higher standard of living, by gathering them together into clergy-houses, and imposing on them a strict rule of life (Chapter IX.) ; how the clergy, thus gathered together in or near the bishop's own church, came to have a special internal organisation, and a special relation to the other clergy of the diocese (Chapters X. and XI.) ; and finally how the change of organisation impressed itself on the internal structure of church buildings, and how the erection of chancels and chancel screens set the final seal upon that separation of the officers from the rest of the community which, more than anything else, may be said to distinguish the churches of modern from those of primitive times (Chapter XII.)

The first point which will be considered is that great difference between early and later organisation by which, instead of each congregation, or small group of allied congregations, having its complete equipment of Church officers,—bishop, presbyters, and deacons,— bishops ceased to be appointed except in cities or county towns.

The causes of that difference are no doubt to be found in the manner in which the Roman Empire decayed in the provinces of the West. To the original position of the empire in those provinces some parallel may be found in the British rule in India; but the manner of its breaking up is the more difficult to describe because no approximate analogy to it exists. In Gaul and Spain every important city had its colony of Roman settlers, in whose hands were not only the executive and judicial functions of the imperial government, but also, for the most part, the municipal administration. In the empire of the first three centuries the Roman colony formed also the centre of that worship of the Emperor which, rather than the worship of Jupiter and Mars, was the official religion. In the later empire it formed the centre and nucleus of Christianity. Like the British in India, whose bishops in the Presidency towns have been themselves Europeans, surrounded for the most part by a European clergy, the bishops of the chief cities of the provinces of the West were mainly Roman, surrounded by a Roman clergy, and, though they were not without a missionary element, they ministered mainly to the wants of the Roman population. Outside the centres of that population they can hardly be said to have existed. Here and there, on the large estates of Roman owners, there was a chapel for Christian service; but the mass of the Celtic peasantry was unconverted. The familiar word " pagan " or " villager " comes to us from this time, and indicates this feature of it. Christianity was the religion of the governing classes and their immediate dependants; it belonged to the cities and not to the country; it was almost a part of the imperial *régime*.

Upon this state of things came the slowly rolling waves of Teutonic conquest. That conquest was rather an amalgamation of races under a Teutonic king, than a complete subversion of the existing state of society. It was only little by little that the decaying estates passed from the hands of Roman or Celtic to those of Teutonic owners, and that the ancient small free-holders became the vassals of Teutonic lords. The only land that was seized was the public land. The Celts and Romans still formed the mass of the population. They retained their customs and their laws. The framework of the imperial organisation remained without material change. And within that framework two features, the one of German character and the other of German usage, preserved much that was old, and laid the foundation of much that was to come. The one feature was that the Germans loved the country rather than the town, and that consequently, though great estates changed hands, the cities were left for the most part to their former inhabitants. The other feature was that, following their traditional usage, they did not impose their own laws upon the inhabitants of the territories which they conquered, but allowed each race to retain, and to be judged by, its own legal code. The general result was that in the cities was gathered together almost all that survived of Rome; the schools preserved the Roman tongue, the courts preserved Roman law, the Church preserved Roman Christianity. Of all this survival of Roman life, the bishop of the *civitas* was the centre. Round him the aristocracy of the old Roman families naturally gathered. He symbolised to them their past glories and their ancient liberties. He was their refuge in trouble, and their chief shield against oppression. His house was not infrequently the old *prætorium*, the residence of the Roman governor. Even his dress was that of a Roman official. In him the empire still lived. Nor did his position rest only upon sentiment. There was in addition the power which came of judicial status and of wealth. His judicial status arose partly from the fact which has been mentioned, that the Roman law continued to be in force for Romans, and partly from the fact that he was allowed a right of interposition in cases in which widows and orphans were concerned. He came to have a seat side by side with the Teutonic *graf* or *comes*, and ultimately had a jurisdiction of his own. His wealth arose partly from the practice of the Roman landowners, sometimes in default of heirs and sometimes in spite of them, bequeathing their lands to him as the head of the political party to which they belonged; and partly from the growing custom on the part of the non-Roman element in the population, of endowing the Church with property "*in remedium animæ*," *i.e.*, to save their souls. The city bishop thus became in a large number of instances a great landowner. As such he not only was the dispenser of ample charities to the poor, but also had a large number of dependants in the serfs, or slaves, upon the Church lands. He was, in short, a personage of such wealth and power that the Frankish king, Chilperic, is reported to have said more than once, "Absolutely the only persons who reign are the bishops: our [*i.e.* the royal] influence has perished, and is transferred to the bishops of the cities."[1]

The permanent result of this importance and power of the city bishop was, that when the country gradually became christianised, instead of each newly formed community having its complete ecclesiastical organisation, as had been the case in Asia Minor and North Africa, the authority of the city bishop was conceived to

---

[1] Greg. Turon. H. F., 6, 46.

extend over all the communities within the district of which the city was the political centre. For in the fusion of Teutonic with what remained of Roman institutions, the Roman *civitas* was taken as the centre of the Teutonic *gau*, or county, a union of two systems of administration which was aided partly by the fact that even in Roman times the *civitas* had round it a certain area or "territorium" (a term which is occasionally used to designate the bishop's diocese of later times), and partly by the fact that the *gau*, or county, was probably only the revival, or the perpetuation, of an earlier Celtic division. The Roman city had, as a rule, been the chief town of the Celtic clan which inhabited the district; and in many instances, when the empire passed away, its Celtic name revived again, *e.g.*, Autricum became again the (*civitas*) Carnutum, *i.e.*, Chartres; Bibona became again the (*civitas*) Cadurcorum, *i.e.*, Cahors. It was in this way that the diocese, in its modern sense, came to exist; the conception of it was Teutonic, the framework was Roman: in respect of that framework so completely is it a survival of the

Roman administration of the West that, even if no other outlines of that administration remained, they could be recovered by tracing those of the ecclesiastical organisation of the Middle Ages.

In Germany and England the system of assigning large districts to a single bishop had another cause. In those countries the Roman administration had had a feebler hold; the colonies of Roman Christians were fewer in number and of less importance : it is probable that Christianity was chiefly spread by the Roman legionaries and their camp followers, and that it hardly existed outside the camps or garrison towns. The result was that when the Roman power died, Christianity also, to a great extent, faded away: though there were bishops in both Germany and Britain, it is extremely doubtful whether they were diocesan bishops in anything like the later sense. The diocesan system of Germany dates from the time of Boniface in the eighth century, and that of England from the time of Theodore in the seventh. The bishops of both countries were in the first instance missionary bishops.

A large tract of country was assigned to them, as it is now assigned to bishops in Africa or India, for the purpose of evangelisation; and when it was christianised the influence of the system which had established itself in Gaul spread both over the Rhine and across the Channel. The example furnished by Gaul, or Frankland as it had by this time become, prevented the subdivision of those bishoprics as the population became christianised. In place of the subdivision of bishoprics grew up the system of archdeaconries and rural deaneries, which continues in the Church of England to the present day.[1]

It has, no doubt, been sometimes maintained that the diocese in its modern sense is an institution of primitive times. But the recorded facts are far from supporting this view. They show that, in the large majority of cases, a

---

[1] There is hardly any trustworthy account of the earliest organisation of the churches of our own country except that which is contained in the small tract of Loofs *Antiquæ Britonum Scotorumque ecclesiæ quales fuerint mores:* London (Nutt), 1882. The history of the English Church prior to the Norman Conquest has yet to be written by an impartial historian.

bishop, presbyters, and deacons existed for every Christian community. As a rule, a city had but a single community, and consequently a single organisation. The officers were officers not of a district but of a community. Where there was more than one community in a city, there was, as a rule, more than one bishop (the decisive passage on this point is Epiphanius, *Hæres.*, lxviii., c. 7, who says that "Alexandria never had two bishops as the other cities had"). At Rome, where the great size of the community prevented its meeting together in a common place of worship, the sense of oneness was preserved by the practice of having only one consecration of the Eucharistic elements, and sending them round by the hands of messengers to the other congregations; and at Rome also it is probable that the Christians in some of the outlying villages in the Campagna were regarded as parts of the one Roman community. At Alexandria the communities of the suburbs and of the adjoining district of the Mareotis were no doubt regarded in some sense independent of, though subordinate to, the city bishop; and, so far, Alexandria may be said to furnish the earliest example of a modern diocese. In Syria also there were communities which had not a complete organisation, and which, like the outlying stations of a modern Wesleyan circuit, were only visited from time to time by the chief officer to whom the oversight of a district was entrusted. But these exceptional cases do not vitiate the inference which the mass of facts forces upon us, that in the greater part of the Christian world each community was complete in itself. Every town, and sometimes every village, had its bishop.

All this is so much at variance with the system of the Western Church in later times, and especially with that of the Church of England, as to be hardly credible except upon the clearest evidence. The diocesan system as it now exists is the effect of a series of historical circumstances. It is impossible to defend every part of it as being primitive, nor is it necessary to do so. It is sufficient to show that it is the result of successive readaptations of the Church's framework to the needs of the times. Behind those readaptations we may properly believe that the Holy Spirit has been working. It is not necessary to believe that His action in all ages is absolutely uniform. If the history of the mediæval, which in all important respects is also the modern, diocese be read by the light of ordinary history, it will be seen to be as clear an instance as could be found of the truth to which in these pages we must again and again refer, that God works with an economy of power, and that the phenomena of the Christian societies are the results of the operation of forces which He has planted for wide and varied purposes in the hearts of men.

*THE DIOCESAN BISHOP.*

## II.

### *THE DIOCESAN BISHOP.*

IT has been shown in the preceding chapter how it came about that the organisation of the Christian communities in the West did not follow the lines of Africa and the East; and that, instead of each newly formed community having its full complement of officers, there were but few bishops outside the cities or county towns. The next point is to show how it came about that the chief officers of one community, *i.e.*, the city bishops, came to have control over the officers of other communities, *i.e.*, the presbyters and deacons in villages and country towns; in other words, how the congregational system of early Christianity passed into the diocesan system of mediæval and modern times.

The common hypothesis is that the officers

of newly formed communities were detached from the bishop's church, and that they preserved the relation of subordination which had attached to them in their original community. But this hypothesis covers only a small proportion of the facts. It is clear that there were 'chapels of ease' in the suburbs of some cities, and mission stations in some outlying country parts; it is clear also that missionaries to the great unconverted Teutonic races retained some kind of allegiance to the church or monastery which had sent them out; but it is clear also that in the greater part of Gaul and Spain the majority of the communities in villages and country towns recognised, or came to recognise, no ecclesiastical superior. For, as a rule, such communities had come into existence under very different conditions from those of the earlier Christian communities, whether in the East or the West. They were not the free associations of Christian colonies who met together, and elected their own officers. They were formed by the owners of great estates who, being themselves Romans and Christians, built chapels in which they and their households might worship, and round which the new converts from paganism gradually clustered. Their officers were not elected, but nominated. They were appointed, paid, and dismissed by the owner of the estate on which they served. There was no necessary tie whatever between them and the bishop of the county town.

In earlier times such a system would have been impossible. All officers, whether bishops, presbyters, deacons, or readers, were originally officers of a particular community, and their status was not recognised, except by courtesy, outside that community. The idea that ordination confers not merely *status*, but *character*, and still more the idea that such character is indelible, are foreign to primitive times. A Church officer who travelled with the usual commendatory epistle from the community to which he belonged received in any strange community the honorary privileges, and probably also the allowances from the Church funds, which were assigned in that community to officers of similar rank with his own. The recognition of each other's officers was, in fact, one of the chief characteristics and advantages of intercommunion. But the recognition was honorary only. The transference of the officer of one Church to another was at first sternly repressed, and afterwards conceded only under stringent limitations. When allowed, it involved reappointment, or, as it would now be called, reordination. Gradually, and by the operation of causes that can be traced, there grew up a conception of the nature of ecclesiastical office which regarded the officers of a particular community as being officers also of the whole body of associated communities. This led to the practice of ordaining persons *absoluté*, *i.e.*, independently of any particular Church. The practice was abused and consequently forbidden; but, though forbidden, it continued to exist: in the seventh and eighth centuries the number of unattached clergy became very large, and it was by them that the detached communities of country districts and the chapels on the estates of private owners were mainly served.

It seems as though there was for a time a real conflict between the system of congregational independence and that of centralised episcopal supervision. From the point of view of those who were acquainted with the canons of the Eastern councils it was a time of anarchy. The danger was the greater because Arian opinions were abroad; and with Arian opinions there was also a relaxation of the stricter moral code of the Catholic world. The picture which is given in the correspondence of Boniface with Pope Zachary shows how grave were the apprehensions of one to whom not only Catholic organisation, but also Catholic faith and morals, were dear. " The pseudo-priests are much more numerous than Catholic priests; there are heretical pretenders, calling themselves bishops and presbyters, who never were ordained by any Catholic bishop, deluding the people, confusing and disturbing the ministries of the Church; there are false vagrants, adulterers, murderers, effeminate sacrilegious hypocrites; there are treasured slaves who have run away from their masters, slaves of the devil transforming themselves into ministers of Christ; who, living as they please, without the control of a bishop, and having influential men as their protectors against bishops to prevent their wicked ways from being stopped, form separate congregations of the people who agree with them, and exercise their heretical ministry not in a Catholic Church, but in country places, in the cottages of peasants, where their uneducated folly may be concealed from the bishops."[1]

It is obvious that if such a state of things had continued the faith and discipline of Western Christendom would have been very different from what they have come to be. Though it is with discipline rather than with faith that we are at present concerned, it is pertinent to point out that the victory which was ultimately won was a victory not only of centralisation over independency, but also of Catholicism over Arianism. For both faith and discipline the crisis was supreme; and it is of singular importance to note that the reformation which shaped the history of the West in all subsequent centuries was effected, under God, by the co-operation of Church and State,

---

[1] Letter of Pope Zachary, in A.D. 748, printed in the collections of St. Boniface's letters, *e.g.*, in Jaffé, *Monumenta Moguntina*, p. 187.

directly by the legislation of the Frankish princes, indirectly by the influence of the see of Rome. The time was singularly favourable for such a co-operation. On the one hand, the reign of the Merovingians was coming to an end, and their successors needed the moral support of the Church ; they could not reckon on the permanence of their alliance with the landed aristocracy ; they needed some abiding internal bond of cohesion for the heterogeneous elements which they were endeavouring to weld into a national unity ; and they found such a bond in the restoration of the decaying organisation of the Frankish Churches. On the other hand, the position of the bishops of Rome, in face of the declining power of the Exarchate of Ravenna and the aggression of the Lombard kings, needed the material support which, at the time, only the Frankish princes could give. Both the co-operation itself, and the form which it took, were due to the enthusiasm and genius of our great countryman Boniface. To him more than to any other single cause the main features of the ecclesiastical system of the West are due ; and from the lines of diocesan episcopacy which he laid down there was not until the Reformation any considerable departure.

Those lines were in the main the revival of some elements of the Eastern system, which is found in its most perfect form in the canons of Chalcedon. The knowledge of that system was probably due to Theodore of Tarsus, who, seventy years before, had reformed and reorganised the Church of England. Boniface had been born probably about the very year (A.D. 680) in which, at the Council of Hertford, Theodore had first brought the Eastern canons into the West, and the years of his early education in the south of England coincided with the first freshness of the revived ideal. It was consequently natural that when, towards the close of his life, he was summoned by Karlman to help in the reform of the Frankish Church, he should have had Theodore's system before his mind. However this may be, the fact that the system which Boniface established was not indigenous in the West, but a revival, after a long period of comparative lapse, of an Eastern type, is of considerable significance.

It is the more deserving of attention because of the common tendency to infer an identity between Eastern and Western usages, and a continuity of existence between the usages of the fifth century and those of the eighth, which is not only wanting in historical proof, but contrary to historical analogy.

The precise means by which the new system was framed and enacted will be variously described as ecclesiastical, or civil, or both, according to the point of view of the narrator. The enactments are to be found, without variation of phrase, in the collections of Church councils and in those of Frankish laws; they are quoted sometimes as ecclesiastical canons, and sometimes as civil "capitularies." The preamble, in almost all cases in which it has survived, recites that they were made by the head of the State, with the joint advice of clergy and laity. It may be added that although both State and Church joined in prescribing and enforcing them, the frequent repetition of some of the more important enactments in successive meetings shows that they were but tardily obeyed.

The main features of the new system have been so strongly marked on the face of Christendom for more than eleven hundred years, as to make it difficult for most persons to conceive of a time when they did not exist. They have again and again been treated as part of the essence of all Christian organisation, and departures from them have been treated as violations of Apostolic order. Their historical origin consequently both requires and deserves a careful examination; and it would be difficult to point out a more instructive collection of data for the history of ecclesiastical organisation than the collections of capitularies in the *Monumenta Germaniæ Historica*, as edited either by Pertz or by Boretius. The features in question are two: (1) the subordination of the clergy of a district to the bishop of the county town or chief city of the district; (2) the co-ordination of the bishops of a province into a single body, with the bishop of the metropolis of the province at their head. Of the second of these features I propose to speak in a subsequent chapter, confining myself at present to the first.

The enactments which bear upon it are complementary of each other : one series enacts that a city bishop shall have jurisdiction over the whole area of which the city was the political centre ; the other series enacts that the presbyters within that area shall recognise his jurisdiction. Both series of enactments are extensions of principles which had hitherto been but imperfectly developed. In the earlier Christian communities presbyters were subordinate not so much to the bishop as to the whole body of their colleagues; and even in the seventh century a Council of Seville[1] had restored to office a presbyter who had been deposed by the bishop without the consent of his council. But henceforth the city bishop had a personal authority over the presbyters of a district. The canons of the Eastern councils had been revived, and the bishop was their conservator. To him the presbyters were responsible ; and the presumption that this responsibility was a new feature of ecclesiastical administration is confirmed by two facts :

---

[1] 6 *Conc. Hispal.*, A.D. 619, c. 6.

(1) that it was enforced by an oath and therefore made to assume the form not of an inherent or statutory right, but of a contract; and (2) that Lull, the successor of Boniface in the see of Mainz, in complaining of two presbyters who had refused obedience to him, makes that obedience rest on a decree of the pope to whom he was writing.[1]

These general enactments were supplemented and enforced by provisions for active supervision. It was required, on the one hand, that every presbyter should report himself once a year to his bishop, and, on the other hand, that the bishop should once a year visit every presbyter's church. Both of these requirements had already existed in some parts of the West, and they were both intended partly as guarantees against the use of heretical practices in the administration of the sacraments, and partly as securities for the preservation of the rights of the bishop in regard to baptism. The former

---

[1] "Cognita enim canonum auctoritate *decrevistis* ut omnes presbyteri qui in parrochia sunt sub potestate episcopi esse debeant."—Lulli, *Epist. ap. S. Bonifat*, Epist. No. 114, *Mon. Mogunt.*, p. 279.

of them was specially intended to secure the right of the bishop to bless the chrism which was used for anointing in baptism, and the holy oil which was used for anointing the sick. The latter of them had several objects in view, and it has also been more permanent.

(1) The first object was preaching. The functions of presbyters in imperfectly organised communities, as in the city Church, were mainly those of administrators of the sacraments. Preaching was the especial, though not the exclusive, function of the bishop. It was to him and not to the presbyters that the cure of souls was committed; he, and not the presbyters, was the " pastor."

(2) The second object was " confirmation," *i.e.*, the imposition of hands upon the newly baptised. The original theory had been that the whole Church should take part in the admission of a new member, and the presence of the chief officer, for whom certain parts of the rite were reserved, was essential to its validity. Where, as for example in Central Italy, bishops were numerous and dioceses of small extent, it is probable that baptism was

as a rule, performed only at the bishop's church, and that confirmation, as a separate rite, existed only for those cases in which presbyters had baptzied in an emergency. In some of the most ancient rituals, baptism, confirmation, and communion are successive stages in a single ceremony. But this had become impossible in the great country districts, with scattered and detached communities, with an imperfect organisation, and with constant accessions of new converts from paganism. It was impracticable that all the new candidates for baptism should make an Easter pilgrimage to the county town. Consequently that which was elsewhere exceptional became the rule. The part of the baptismal rite which was ordinarily performed by presbyters and deacons was performed by them, without the presence of a bishop, in a "baptismal," or, as it would now be termed, a "parish," church. The part which was ordinarily performed by a bishop, and which in the West, though not in the East, had come to be considered an inalienable function of the episcopal office, was postponed until the bishop's annual visit. The laying on of hands thus came to assume the additional importance which attached to a distinct ceremony, and was ultimately elevated to the rank of a separate sacrament.

(3) The third object was discipline. This was partly a continuation of the disciplinary functions of the officers of the primitive Churches, with the important difference, that whereas in primitive times the bishop was only the president of a disciplinary council, in later times he acted alone. There are indeed traces that even in his visitations the presbyters of a district were at first associated with him, forming a local court analogous to the court which was formed by the bishop and presbyters in a city; but these traces are infrequent, and at last altogether disappear. For concurrently with this continuation of primitive functions there was an extension to country districts of the judicial functions which under the later imperial administration, and afterwards under the fusion of the imperial with the Teutonic administrations, had become attached to the office of a city bishop. The two kinds of functions are often confused, and require to

be distinguished from each other. It is important to note that, from the time of Charles the Great, a bishop on his visitation tour acted in a double capacity, partly as an officer of the Church, preserving the ancient tradition of ecclesiastical discipline, and partly as an officer of the State, exercising powers with which the State had armed him. In the former capacity he was properly the colleague of his presbyters; in the latter he acted alone. But the latter capacity so far overshadowed the former that the primitive tribunal of bishop and presbyters ceased to exist. The bishop in his visitation acted, in fact, as a commissioner of the government, vested with an authority which was precisely analogous to that of the other commissioners by whom Charles supplemented the action of the central authority, and whose existence has left its trace in our own time and country in the judges of assize. The bishop in his visitation was commonly invested with a commission to inquire into cases of murder, adultery, and other wrongdoings "which are contrary to the law of God, and which Christian men ought to avoid." He was, above all, to stamp out the remains of paganism. He was to be an active agent in carrying out the great policy of establishing a Christian empire. In doing so he was not merely to adjudge cases which might be brought before him, but also to inquire into the existence of such cases. He was, in fact, to begin that system of "inquisition" which, however innocent in its original intention, afterwards filled a dark page in the history of Christianity. The weapon with which he was armed was in the first instance the legitimate ecclesiastical weapon of excommunication. Any one who was found to be guilty of flagrant immorality, or of practising pagan rites, was excluded from the Church. And if the ecclesiastical weapon failed of its effect, the bishop might resort to the "secular arm." In any case the king's officers were bound to help him; and a determined resistance to his sentence involved the severest penalties of the civil law.

Such was the origin of modern diocesan episcopacy. It grew up in the Frankish domain, under the legislation of the Frankish princes and kings, by the co-operation of Church and State, at the instigation in the first instance of the great missionary Boniface. For some time previously the Churches in outlying districts had had no recognised ecclesiastical superior. They were now made subject to the bishop of the county town, and the bishop was required to exercise over them an active supervision. It is probable that at the time no other system was possible. It is certain that, at least for the time, the system was an enormous gain. Whatever be its merits or demerits in its abstract relation to Christianity, it must at least be credited with the great work of having saved the Churches of the West from a disintegration which would have involved for the clergy a revival of Arianism, and for the masses of the people a relapse into paganism.

*THE FIXED TENURE OF THE PARISH
PRIEST.*

## III.

### *THE FIXED TENURE OF THE PARISH PRIEST.*

THE gradual formation in the villages and country towns of Western Europe of churches with imperfect organisations, which stood at first in no direct relation to the bishops' churches in the old Roman municipalities, altered in several material respects the conditions under which ecclesiastical offices were held. In the original organisation, even after it had been modified by the transference to the bishop, or to the body of the clergy, of many of the proper functions of the whole community, the officers of a church were appointed, or, in the later phrase, " ordained," to their positions in that church. They could not leave it except under special circumstances. The loss of office in it meant loss of office altogether, nor could they lose office except by the action of the body of which they were members. But when, after the breaking up of the Imperial system, the tie which bound each officer to his own church was loosened or broken, and the principle, "Once a presbyter, always a presbyter," came to prevail; when the officers of the communities which grew up independently of the bishop's church were not elected by the community, or ordained specially to an office in it, but nominated by the founder of the church or the owner of the estate on which it was built, the admission to church office and the deposition from it proceeded upon altogether different lines. The owner of a church building claimed and exercised the right of appointing and dismissing its ministers at his pleasure and without reference to any other authority. In the city churches the ancient rule remained; their officers were appointed by the bishop with the approval of his council and of the whole community; and when once appointed they could not lose their office except for misconduct. In the country churches, on the contrary, they were simply the servants of the owner, who might pay them what he pleased, and send them away when he pleased, with or without good cause.

It is proposed in the present chapter to show how the rights or claims of owners in this respect came to be limited, how a parish priest came to have a fixity of tenure, and how the modern rights of patronage are in their origin not a usurpation by owners of the rights of the Church, but a limitation by the Church of the rights of owners.

It must be remembered that the mass of country churches were not, in the modern sense of the term, consecrated, and that those who had built them retained over them the same right of ownership which they had over other buildings on their estates. They could sell, alienate, or destroy them. They appointed officers to them as they appointed farm-bailiffs. There was no right of interference, either ecclesiastical or civil. It is obvious that in such cases discipline was impossible. There was no guarantee for either soundness of faith or purity of morals if a man's appointment to and tenure of office depended not upon the bishop, but upon the landlord. The assertion of some kind of ecclesiastical control was a vital necessity. Just as no one could be appointed to the grade of priest or deacon without the intervention of a bishop, so it became necessary to insist on the intervention of a bishop when a priest or deacon was appointed to minister in a particular church. But the attempt to insist on it was stoutly resisted. There is probably no regulation which in the course of the earlier Middle Ages required such frequent re-enactment, and which shows, by the fact of such re-enactment, that it was constantly broken. Charles the Great endeavoured to treat the matter with a strong hand :—

"Let Your Utility be aware," he writes in a circular letter or edict to his vassals and administrative officers, " that there has resounded in our ears an enormous presumption of some of you that you do not obey your bishops as the authority of the laws and canons requires; I mean that, with incredible temerity, you refuse to present presbyters to bishops : nay, more, you do not shrink from taking other men's clerks, and venture to put them into your churches without the bishop's consent. . . . We therefore bid and require that no one whatever of our vassals, from the least to the greatest, venture to be disobedient to his bishop in things which pertain to God. . . . If any one take an opposite course, let him know that without doubt, unless he speedily amends his ways, he will give an account thereof in our presence."[1]

But the rights of property, as they were then conceived, were stronger than even the strong arm of the emperor. Seven times was the rule re-enacted in the latter years of his reign and in the reign of his son; and it reappears even so late as the eleventh century in France, Germany, and England.

There were several sides to the regulation. In the first place, from the point of view of ecclesiastical discipline, it was an assertion of the claim of the main body of Christians in a district, as represented by their chief officer, to

---

[1] *Karoli Epistola in Italian missa*, Boretius, p. 203: *Edictum pro episcopis*, Pertz, i., p. 81; also printed among the *Epistolæ Carolinæ*, No. 17 in Jaffé, *Mon. Carolina*, p. 371.

control the officers of particular congregations; it was a denial of the right of Separatists or Nonconformists to exist. In the second place, it was a limitation of the rights of the owners of property which had been dedicated to religious purposes. In the third place, it was a safeguard for the ministers of a church against the caprice or the injustice of those whom, by anticipation, we may call their "patrons;" it tended to give them "fixity of tenure."

In modern times this fixity of tenure is combined with a freehold right in both the church itself and its revenues. Such a freehold right in the church is of much later growth than the earlier Middle Ages. Its non-existence in the earlier Middle Ages is manifest by abundant evidence. For example, (1) there are many surviving documents in which men deal with churches in precisely the same way as they deal with their other property; they describe them as their own churches or the churches of their family property ("propria ecclesia," "ecclesia propriæ hereditatis"); they bequeath them either absolutely or with limitations, sometimes to one person and sometimes to several persons. (2) There are express and repeated enactments which recognise these rights of owners—*e.g.*, "Churches which have been built by freemen may be transferred or sold, provided only that the church be not destroyed."[1] (3) Church writers of the time mention with regret not only that churches themselves were sold, but that also the gifts of several generations of the faithful were sold with them.[2]

But although it was not until about the twelfth century that the ministers of a parish church began to have a right of property in the church itself, they began to claim and to enjoy at a much earlier period a right to its revenues. The right was not conceded as a matter of course. The Roman law, which recognised the Christian communities as corporations with the right of holding property and disposing of it, recognised only a single community in each city. The churches which were built within the "territorium" of a city had no rights distinct from the bishop's church; the churches

---

[1] *Capit. Francofurt.*, A.D. 794, c. 54.
[2] *E.g.*, Agobard of Lyons, *De dispensatione divinarum rerum*, c. 15, in Migne, *Patrol. Lat.*, vol. civ., p. 237.

which were built by private persons on their own land were as much their own property as were the barns or cottages. The German occupation of Roman lands did not change in this respect the legal status of either the bishop's church or other churches. The Roman law continued to be of force. Indeed, it is probable that the Germans had no precedent or rule for the holding of property by what we should now call " spiritual corporations." That is to say, the bishop's church continued to hold its property because it was governed by Roman law; the country churches could not hold property because neither in Roman nor in German law was there any precedent for their doing so.

The history of the rights of parish churches is the history of the assertion of a double claim, on the one hand that of the church as a whole against private owners, on the other hand that of parish churches against the bishop.

The first of these claims seems to have successfully asserted itself in the sixth and seventh centuries. It is first found in the decrees of Spanish councils. The Second Council of

FIXED TENURE OF THE PARISH PRIEST. 51

Braga (A.D. 572, c. 6) speaks of persons building churches on their property expressly that they might share in the offerings, and strongly forbids bishops to consecrate churches so built. The Fourth Council of Toledo (A.D. 633, c. 33) tells founders of churches that they have no rights in the property of the churches which they have founded, but that the disposal of it belongs to the bishop. The later canon law on the point is based on a letter of Gregory the Great to Felix of Messina, in which he expressly denies to the owner any right in the church, except the right of admission " which is due to all Christians in common."[1]

The second claim had a longer history, which must be traced in greater detail.

The bishop had been from the earliest times the chief administrator of Church property. Even if it be not true that such administration was in the primitive Church his primary function, it is demonstrably true that when Christianity was recognised by the State, and

---

[1] S. Greg., *M. Epist.*, 2. 5, ad Felic. Messan. (quoted by Gratian, c. 26, Caus. XVI., qu. 7, as from Gelasius).

the churches were made capable of holding property, it was regarded as an inherent and important part of his office. When country churches began to receive gifts of land, the city bishop was the only person who could legally hold them. In some cases he was not slow to claim them. However strongly a man might desire to specially benefit the church of his own district, and however much the ministers of such a church might need support, the city bishop was legally entitled to claim whatever was offered. The most conclusive evidence of this is that which is afforded by the Council of Carpentras in A.D. 527. "A complaint has reached us," say the Acts of that council, " that the offerings which are bestowed by certain of the faithful on parish churches are so taken possession of by some bishops that little or nothing is left to the churches on which they were bestowed ; it seems to us to be fair and reasonable that if the church of the city over which the bishop presides is so well supplied that, by the favour of Christ, it does not want anything, the offerings to parish churches should reasonably be allotted to the clergy of those churches, or for their repair; if, on the other hand, it appears that the bishop has many expenses and but little property, only so much should be reserved for the parish churches as is reasonably sufficient for the clergy, or for their repair, and the bishop should claim the surplus for himself." This canon fully recognises the legal right of the bishop, but it marks the transition to the later state of things in its recommendation that the exercise of that right should be limited to cases in which the necessities of his church required it. But the reasonable course which this canon recommends was not always taken. A hundred years later the Fourth Council of Toledo (A.D. 633, c. 33) applies to the action of bishops in the matter the apostolic words, "Avarice is the root of all evils." "Many of the faithful, for the love of Christ and the martyrs, build churches in the dioceses of bishops, and endow them with offerings, but the bishops take the offerings away and convert them to their own uses; the consequence is that the ministers fail, since they lose their means of support, and the ruins of decaying churches are not repaired." Twenty-two years later a council of the same province (the Ninth Council of Toledo, c. i.) took the stronger course of empowering the heirs of the founder of a church to watch over the proper appropriation of its funds, and to bring an avaricious bishop before the metropolitan or the king.

But gradually, and before the last-mentioned councils, a rule had been growing up that the bishop should have a *third* of the revenues of parishes. There are many traces of the rule in subsequent times, but there is not enough evidence to show to what extent it was generally observed. In North Italy at the beginning of the ninth century there was an express enactment against giving any part of the tithes of parishes to the bishop; but the custom is found several years later on the Rhine and in France. At the great ecclesiastical conference of Worms in 829, and also in the Council of Paris in the same year, the right of the bishop to a fourth, not a third, of parish churches is recognised; but the bishops are urged to remit their share unless they are in special need of it.[1] Like

---

[1] Pertz., M.G.H., i., p. 335, c. 5; 6 Conc. Paris., c. 31.

almost all attempts to fix an unvarying rule for constantly varying circumstances, this attempt to give the bishop a definite share in the property of outlying churches became unworkable. The growing importance and wealth of most city churches made such a share unnecessary as part of a bishop's revenue; and at the same time the extinction of the remains of paganism, the inclusion of almost all the inhabited parts of the West in the network of the parochial system, and the consequent large increase in the number of the parochial clergy, provided ample channels for the expenditure of the local funds in the localities from which they were derived. The fixed ratio of revenues was replaced by presents in recognition of the bishop's rights. Such presents tended to be rather involuntary than voluntary, and not unfrequently became oppressive exactions. Sometimes they were forbidden by law, and sometimes they were regulated; for example, in the Parliament which was held by Charles the Bald at Toulouse in 844, it was enacted that a bishop should not require from a parish more than a bushel of barley, a keg of wine, and a pig worth six pence, or six pence in lieu of it.[1] In time these payments in kind were all commuted for money fees, and the ancient right of a bishop to a third of all parochial revenues has dwindled in modern times to the payment of small fees to an archdeacon or a bishop on the occasion of his visitation.

In this way the detached congregations, after having been brought into the ecclesiastical system, retained or regained no small amount of liberty; in this way also the ministers of such congregations, after having been brought under the control of the city bishop, obtained, on the one hand, a tenure which was not dependent on the caprice of their patron, and, on the other hand, revenues which were not dependent on the caprice of their bishop. "From the beginning it was not so;" the changed circumstances of Western Europe compelled a change in the relations of ministers to their congregations, and

---

[1] Karoli II., *Synodus apud Tolosam*, c. 2, Pertz, i., p. 378, "unum modium ordei atque unum modium vini . . . et frischingam sex valentem denarios aut sex pro ea denarios:" the whole might be commuted for a payment of "duos solidos."

of congregations to one another. The ecclesiastical system was elastic enough to cover new needs; and, being elastic, it changed its form. The parochial system grew up underneath the cover of the episcopal system, and as an extension of it. The assignment of separate revenues to the separate parishes prevented an accumulation of enormous funds in the hands of the city bishops, which would have been sufficiently dangerous to the State to have brought about their overthrow. The virtual independence of parish ministers, so long as they conformed to general rules, combined the advantages which flow from the multiplication of centres of activity with those which flow from centralised administration. It would be a needless and probably also an untrue optimism to maintain that whatever happened was the ideal best; but it is none the less clear that the result was not an abnormal outgrowth which needed to be uprooted, but a legitimate outcome of the action of the ordinary forces of our moral nature within the Christian sphere.

*THE BENEFICE.*

## IV.

### *THE BENEFICE.*

IN the sixth and seventh centuries the property of the Church in the West had enormously increased. The number of churches and monasteries was multiplied, and every church and monastery came to have property of its own. With the spread of Christianity in the country districts, and also with the tendency on the part of the survivors of Roman families, in the countries which had been most thickly planted with Roman colonies, to make the Church their heir, there grew up a strong revival of the belief that the gift of money to the Church, and thereby to the clergy and the poor, was a sure means of saving the soul. No small proportion of the deeds of grant which remain, and of the " formulæ " or draft forms for such deeds, recite by way of preamble that the grant is made by the donor "for the benefit of my soul, and that I may obtain pardon of my sins." The result was that the Church became the richest landowner in Western Europe.

The modes in which gifts were made to the Church were of various kinds, and as they all have a bearing upon subsequent times, it is necessary to distinguish them from one another.

1. The simplest and most general mode was that of donation in a man's lifetime. This was effected by word of mouth before witnesses ; and a written instrument, though not essential to its validity, yet was a convenient record of the fact. In Teutonic communities it is probable that no other mode of gift was at first recognised by law ; donation to a church by will seems to have no legal effect, and even if it had, the Church naturally preferred an irrevocable gift during a man's life to the uncertainty of a testamentary disposition.

2. Where Roman law prevailed, that is to say, among the descendants of the Roman population, even where Teutonic law was the

general law of the land, donations by will continued to exist. Such donations were revocable during the lifetime of the donor, and seem to have been not always respected after his death, inasmuch as some extant forms of a will bind both the donor and his heirs by a penalty not to revoke or disregard it. In course of time donations by will came to be recognised in Teutonic communities; but the fact of their Roman origin is shown by their being drawn not after Teutonic but after Roman forms of donation; and the fact of their slow recognition is indicated, among other proofs, by the expressions of doubt which Charles the Great referred to his adviser Alcuin.[1]

3. It was probably in consequence of this want of power to prevent revocation during a man's lifetime and of the presumption of Teutonic law in favour of his heirs after his death that a third mode of donation became more frequent than any other, namely, donation with reservation to the donor of the usufruct of the property during his lifetime. It is

---

Alcuini *Epist.*, 253, ed. Jaffé (127, ed. Froben.) in the *Mon. Carolina*, p. 806.

probable that this mode was in the first instance not recognised by law, inasmuch as the element in the transfer of property to which the Northern races attached most importance, and which underlies the modern "induction" of a clerk to his benefice, was necessarily absent from it. But in the extant forms of deed in which property is thus given to the Church there is an express stipulation that the donation shall hold good in spite of the absence of this corporal surrender of the property; and sometimes the donor requires that if his heirs bring a lawsuit for the recovery of the property, they shall pay a heavy fine. Sometimes the legal difficulties of this mode of donation were overcome by making the donation absolute, and adding a petition, which the new owner, that is the Church, was morally, if not legally, bound to grant, that the original owner should continue to enjoy the use of the property without power to alienate it, and with the obligation to keep it in good order.

It was natural that this tendency to endow churches and monasteries with lands on a large scale, and thus to create a power which might be formidable to the State, should meet with checks on the part of the secular authorities. We consequently find that both in the Teutonic codes, and in the adaptations of the civil law which were in force among the Roman element in Teutonic countries, stringent safeguards and limitations were introduced in the interests of a man's family. In some cases the right of donation was limited to those who had no children; in others no donation was valid unless it had received the sanction of the head of the State; any person who had a claim upon an estate had to be consulted before it could be alienated, and if his consent were not obtained, he could bring a suit for its restitution. The existence of this tendency to put difficulties in the way of the acquisition of property by the Church is also shown by the frequent enactments of councils in reference to it. The penalty of excommunication was constantly imposed upon those who so far "despised their own souls" as to endeavour to retain what their relatives had bequeathed to the "servants of God" and the poor.[1]

---

[1] *E.g.*, the Second Council of Lyons, in A.D. 567, c. 1, "de

But in spite of all difficulties and restrictions, the landed property of the Church became enormous. The bishops in a large proportion of cases were the chief landowners in their dioceses. They kept the administration of the property for the most part in their own hands, with the help of a vice-lord, "vicedominus," or "economus," who is frequently mentioned in connection with the archdeacon, the latter being the bishop's deputy in spiritual, as the former was in temporal affairs. The lands were worked by serfs and slaves. Of this there are abounding proofs. The slaves were slaves in the strict sense of the term, "chattels" who passed with the land from one owner to another. It was not until long afterwards that the public opinion of the Church declared itself against slavery in any form ; and it may reasonably be inferred that the condition of church-slaves was easier than that of the slaves of private owners.

---

quibus rebus si quis *animæ suæ contemptor* aliquid alienare præsumpserit, usque ad emendationis suæ vel restitutionis rei ablatæ a consortio ecclesiastico vel omnium Christianorum convivio labeatur alienus " : other similar enactments are Conc. Agath., A.D. 504, c. 4 ; 1 Conc. Arvern., A.D. 535, c. 14 ; 4 Conc. Aurel., A.D. 541, c. 14 ; 3 Conc. Paris, A.D. 557, c. 1.

One reason for this inference is that such slaves could become clerks without the difficulties which impeded the ordination of ordinary slaves. There was probably also a more frequent manumission of such slaves; and their condition when made free was the better because they were under the special protection of the Church to which they had belonged. It may be interesting to quote one of the extant draft forms of manumission :—

"In the name of God, N., though a sinner, yet, by the grace of God, bishop, wishing to obtain the mercy of God, who says, 'Blessed are the merciful, for they shall obtain mercy,' and whose Divine word admonishes us by His prophet, 'Let the oppressed go free and break every burden' (Isa. lviii. 6), with the consent of our brethren and fellow-citizens, . . . have agreed that we ought to pay a tithe of all the slaves of our church. Therefore we set free from the present day M., a slave of our church, whom we know, as the prophet says, to be 'oppressed,' so that from henceforth he may live for himself, act for himself, work for himself, become really free, as if he had been born of free parents, and have granted to him all the property which he either has or can acquire. And, moreover, if he uses the defence and protection of our Church, let him know that it is given him not to impose slavery upon him anew, but to defend him."[1]

As time went on, and the property became still larger, the personal administration of property by bishops became, to a great extent, impracticable. There grew up a system which has left its mark not only upon the whole Western Church, but also upon the whole economical condition of Europe to the present day. It was the system of lending lands, with or without the payment of a rent, and for a definite or indefinite period, to persons who undertook to cultivate them and enjoyed the usufruct of them, and who came to form an intermediate class between the owner and the actual tillers of the soil. The usufruct of church lands was sometimes thus given to laymen and sometimes to clerks. When given to clerks, it was given without the payment of a rent in

---

[1] *Formulæ Bituricenses*, No. 8, in K. Zeumer's *Formulæ Merowingici et Karolini ævi*, pars prior, p. 171.

return: the property was assigned for their maintenance during their lifetime, subject to a power of recall by the bishop in case of their misbehaviour. The clerks were still in theory paid out of the funds of the bishop's church; but instead of receiving money or food, they received a farm. This was the case also with the canons of a cathedral when the canonical system began; and hence the later use of " præbenda," which originally meant " rations," and ultimately was applied to the estate which produced the rations.

When church lands were lent to a layman they were sometimes, even if infrequently, lent without the payment of a rent, but more commonly, and, after the middle of the eighth century, invariably, lent on condition of a rent being paid to the Church. The amount of such rent was often very small; but it was at any rate a recognition of ownership. In some cases the land was thus lent to powerful men to secure their support, or to the relatives of a bishop or abbot as a private favour. The records of the Abbey of Fontenelle, for example, relate that a certain Abbot Teutsind (734—738) gave almost a third of the estates to his relatives and to courtiers.[1] There are deeds extant which provide for the payment of what was obviously the nominal rent of a few pounds of wax ; and the fact that the system was sometimes abused is also indicated by the existence of clauses in deeds of gift providing that the land given shall be used for the benefit of the Church, and shall not be lent by the bishop to secular persons. One of the many survivals of the system in modern times is the payment of rent on saints' days. It was on certain great festivals, and especially the festival of the patron saint, that persons would naturally go from country parts to the central church of the district, and it was, therefore, convenient that on those occasions they should take their rent with them; hence it was that "Lady-day," being the festival of one to whom a large proportion of churches came to be dedicated, became a common rent day.

Sometimes this lending of church lands was not voluntary, but compulsory. The head of

---

[1] *Gesta Abbat. Fontanell.*, c. 10, in Pertz, *M.G.H.*, *Scriptt.*, ii., p. 282.

the State resumed possession of them, and assigned them to his soldiers. In all cases rent was paid for such lands, nor was the proceeding held in the first instance to be objectionable. The most important instance of it was resolved upon at the Council or Parliament of Lestines ("Concilium Liftinense") in 743, at which Boniface was present. Neither he nor Pope Zachary, who wrote on the subject, seem to have complained of it, or considered that it was otherwise than necessary. But by one of those misunderstandings of history which gather force as they roll on, this compulsory tenancy came to be viewed as a robbery; the facts that the exigencies of State were imperative, and that rent was paid for the use of the lands, were forgotten, and the supposed author of the supposed spoliation, Charles Martel, was pictured by the writers of the Middle Ages as undergoing the fiercest of all the tortures of hell.

Land thus rented was said to be held "ad precariam," or "ad beneficium." The essence of a "precaria" was that it was revocable; it was ordinarily renewed on petition every five years, and the ordinary forms of such petition have been preserved. The custom of so renewing it was probably a survival of the Roman custom of renewing the leases of the public land every five years, *i.e.*, with every new " censor," a custom which had continued to exist even after the censorship had ceased to be active, and which seems to have spread also to the lands held by temples or religious societies, *e.g.*, those of the Vestal Virgins. In Roman law there was a distinction between this tenure by "precaria" and tenure by "beneficium;" but the two kinds of tenure did not greatly differ, and in the earlier Middle Ages the two terms were used as convertible. For the custom of renewing by petition gradually died out. A form of grant came to be used which specified that it should be deemed to be renewed from time to time without any process of actual renewal, and this was succeeded by the custom of allowing the beneficial use of land to continue during the lifetime of the beneficiary. It was natural that this system should easily lapse into a system of continuing the lease to a man's heirs. A beneficiary came to look upon his land as passing by a kind

## THE BENEFICE.

of right from father to son; it is clear that in most respects he could do as he pleased with it, the words of the extant deeds " saving the right of the saint " (*i.e.*, the patron saint of the church to which the land belonged) being inserted as the only saving clause.

When, on the contrary, the use of church lands was given to clerks, though they had full legal possession during their lifetime, the lands reverted to the Church at their death.

In course of time the word " beneficium " ousted the word " precaria," and became the common expression which ultimately covered all permanent sources from which church officers derived emolument. It was applied not only to canonries and parish cures, but also to bishoprics and the popedom itself. Its main interest for us is in its relation to parishes; and the history of that relation is especially deserving of study, now that the whole question of the endowments of the Church is coming into the field of active discussion. The history is necessarily complicated, inasmuch as it not only covers a large period of time, but also embraces many various elements of different systems of law. But although it is complex, the following distinctions will perhaps help to make it clear:—

1. Sometimes a bishop assigned part of the lands which had been given to him or to his church to the church of a particular locality, or, in other words, to a parish. In such cases there was no one to interfere with his free right to nominate as the minister of that church, and consequently as the holder of the lands so assigned, any clerk whom he pleased. This came to be technically known as "collatio libera," and afterwards simply as "collatio." The clerk so presented held the lands so assigned as a "beneficium" of which he had full legal possession, but which reverted at his death to the bishop who had presented him.

2. Sometimes lands were assigned in a similar way by other persons, especially by the owners of the land on which a church had been built. In the first instance, churches so built, as has been previously mentioned, were regarded as being as much a man's own property as were farm-buildings: the owner

appointed whomsoever he pleased to minister, and assigned him what funds he pleased for his support. In the second stage of the history, the owner was compelled to present any one whom he so nominated as minister to the bishop of the central town of the district. In the third stage, the right of ownership was further limited by the growing practice of formally setting apart the churches built upon private lands for the service of God, in other words of "consecrating" them. In the next stage, there grew up with the practice of consecration the practice of requiring that a church, before being consecrated, should have a permanent source of income sufficient for the support of its presbyter. The most common of such requirements was that of "unus *mansus* integer," *mansus* being, in the land-measure of the time, a plot of ground sufficient to support one person besides the two serfs who were employed to cultivate it. In the first instance the owner of the land upon which the church was built, and of the lands which before its consecration were assigned for its support, *i.e.*, in the language of early mediæval law the "patronus," or "senior" (of which terms "patron" has almost exclusively survived in England, and "seigneur" in France), not only nominated a clerk to the benefice, but also "inducted" him when the bishop's consent to his nomination had been given. In this fact lay the roots of the great "investiture" controversy of the eleventh and twelfth centuries. In the final stage, the rights of private owners in regard to the induction, or, as it was otherwise termed, the "investiture" of a clerk, passed to the bishop, who thereby became, in the strict sense, the feudal lord of all the benefices in his diocese. The rights of the owner came to be limited to simple nomination; when the clerk whom he had nominated was accepted by the bishop, the rights of the owner were in fact suspended until the next vacancy. The homage which was paid for ecclesiastical as for other benefices was paid, not to him, but to the bishop; the oath of obedience which a secular lord exacted from his vassal was exacted by a bishop from the holders of benefices in his diocese; and the feudal relation of a bishop to his beneficed clergy came almost altogether to supersede the original spiritual relation of ordainer and ordained.

It was by these complex processes, and by the slow evolution of time, that the modern ecclesiastical benefice came into being. In it probably more than in any other existing institution the forms and features of feudalism survive. If it be not apostolic or even primitive, it at least belongs to a great series of historical growths which cannot be wholly set aside, either on the ground that the conditions which gave rise to them have ceased to exist, or on the gound that there are areas of human life in which they fail to do useful work. On the other hand, the fact that the phases through which the institution has passed have been many in number, and various in kind, may properly suggest the question whether, now that the present phase has lasted for several centuries, and also now that modern life has altered some of the conditions under which that phase was formed, there may not be desirable modifications of it which, without altering its essence or breaking the historical continuity of its life, may yet give it a new force for our modern needs, and thereby a new strength for accomplishing the work which the Church has yet to do in the human society of both the present and the future.

*THE PARISH.*

## V.

### *THE PARISH.*

THE word parish (παροικία) originally meant a "sojourning." It is applied in the New Testament (Acts xiii. 17), as it is constantly applied in the Septuagint version of the Old Testament, to the sojourning of the Jews in Egypt. By a natural and not uncommon transition of meaning, it came to be used, in a concrete sense, of a colony of sojourners in the midst of an alien population, such as the Jews were in all the great cities of the Roman Empire. It came hence to be used of the early Christian communities. The Christians of Rome or Corinth formed a colony of sojourners. The only uncertainty which attaches to the use of the word in its relation to Christians is whether it was simply a transference from its similar use in relation to the

Jews, or whether the early Christians may not also have used it, as St. Peter uses it (1 Peter i. 17; compare ii. 11), of the temporary and transitory life on earth in contrast to the abiding life of heaven.

The παροικία was thus not a local area, but an aggregate of persons. It does not appear to have been applied to a local area until the Church was fully organised, and it was then applied to the area over which a bishop presided, that is to say, to what is now called a "diocese." Such transitions of meaning are not uncommon in the history of language, and the term so far presents no special difficulty. Its application to smaller areas of ecclesiastical jurisdiction, to a "parish" in its modern sense, is a more complicated question, and one which does not admit of a ready answer. The points which have been considered in previous chapters, the building of churches which were not bishops' churches, in towns and country districts, the endowment of such churches with money and lands, the union of the churches of a county in common subordination to the bishop of the county town, are far from accounting for the phenomenon which begins to present itself in the earlier part of the Middle Ages, each that of such churches was conceived to have a definite area of jurisdiction.

There is a preliminary question which is not without interest. How was it that the conception of such an arrangement came to exist? How was it that the farmers and peasantry who resorted to a certain building for common worship came not only to consider themselves as forming a distinct ecclesiastical society, but also to regard the district in which they lived as being attached by a special tie to the building in which they worshipped? It is probable that the idea came into Christianity from outside.[1] Grimm shows that in pre-Christian Germany districts were attached to heathen temples. Von Maurer in his account of the conversion of the Norse races says that in Iceland, in heathen times, not only was the leader of a new settlement bound to set apart land for a temple, but also the inhabitants of the settlement were bound to maintain the

---

[1] *Deutsche Mythologie*, 2te Ausg., Bd. i., 76.

temple, and to provide the wherewithal for the sacrifices.[1] The inference is that the idea of the mediæval and modern parish is Teutonic in its origin, and the inference is corroborated by the fact that parishes are first found in Teutonic lands. They have sometimes been traced, like many other ecclesiastical institutions, to Rome. But the Roman institution of "tituli" is of another kind. The essence of that institution was not the formation of definite areas of administration and jurisdiction, but rather the assignment of certain churches to certain presbyters, and of certain funds to certain churches. The only early division of Rome into ecclesiastical areas was its division into seven wards or "regions," one of which was assigned to each of the seven deacons, for purposes of charitable relief. There is an even less tenable theory, which supposes that it was an early practice for most bishops to parcel out their dioceses into districts, as an Act of Parliament parcels out England into separate and clearly defined

---

[1] *Die Bekehrung des Norwegischen Stammes zum Christenthum*, Bd. i., 239; cf. *Geschichte des Dorfverfassung in Deutschland*, Bd. i., 110.

areas for local government or parliamentary voting ; but this theory is a mere guess, and so far from being supported by recorded facts, is altogether inconsistent with them.

But although the basis of the arrangement had been laid in Teutonic lands by pre-Christian agencies, the superstructure is wholly Christian, and may be traced mainly to the operation of two sets of causes, that is, partly to the regulations respecting the celebration of baptism, and partly to the regulations respecting the payment of tithes.

In early times and in the great city churches baptism had been an important function. It was ordinarily celebrated only once a year. The whole organised community, bishops, presbyters, deacons, and people, took part in it. In the disorganisation which had taken place in the Transalpine countries of the West, two things had happened in respect to it. In the first place, the elaborate ceremonial had almost wholly passed away, and the liberty which had once been exceptional had become the rule, that it might be celebrated at any time and anywhere. In the second place, Arian practices prevailed so widely, and Arian clergy were so numerous in country districts, that Arian rather than Catholic baptism had become very general. There was a consequent call for regulations which should, on the one hand, restore the old ceremonial and limit the use of it to certain seasons, and, on the other hand, afford some guarantee that the Catholic formula should be used. With the second of these regulations we are not now immediately concerned; the first of them has an important bearing on the history of parishes.

The regulation took the form of requiring that baptisteries should only exist in places in which the bishop appointed them. It was first made in one of the earliest councils of the Carlovingian Reformation, that which was held by Pippin at Vernon, in Normandy, in 755.[1] The regulation had the effect of dividing all churches outside the bishop's own church into two classes, those in which baptisms could be performed and those in which they could not. In some respects the history of baptismal

---

[1] *Conc. Vernense*, c. 7; Pertz, i., 24; Boretius, p. 34.

churches for the following half-century is obscure; when they reappear into the clear light they do so in connection with tithes. It is evident that baptismal churches claimed a superior importance over the other country churches; it is also evident that they claimed a share in the newly sanctioned payment of tithes. It was natural that they should begin to assert a special independence; and we find a royal enactment in Lombardy in 803 to the effect that henceforward no part of the tithe which was paid to a baptismal church should go to the bishop's church.[1] Shortly afterwards we find a regular form of deed for the constitution and endowment of such churches; in it a bishop states that certain villages ought to look to a certain church for masses, baptism, and preaching, and that they ought to give their tithes to that church; he also endows the church from the general lands of the diocese with what would now be called a glebe.[2] Such churches came to have a public

---

[1] *Capit. Langobard*, c. 10; Pertz, i., 110; *Capitulare Mantuanum*, Boretius, p. 195.

[2] De Rozière, *Recueil de Formules*, DLXIV., tom. ii. p. 705.

character, and to be more sharply distinguished from the class of churches out of which they had originally grown, and which still continued to exist side by side with them, churches on private property which belonged to private owners. One point of distinction between them is repeatedly insisted upon, namely, that the rectors of baptismal churches must be presbyters, and not deacons or clerks of lower grade; the other and chief point of distinction was that baptismal churches came more and more to claim the tithes of the district which surrounded them. Exactly a century after the Council of Vernon, a council or parliament which was held by Lewis II. at Pavia recites the complaint of the clergy that "some laymen who have churches on their own property . . . do not give their tithes to the churches where they receive baptism, preaching, confirmation, and the other sacraments of Christ, but assign them at their own pleasure to their own churches and their own clerks."[1] The complaint was listened to, and the distinction

---

[1] Hludowici II., *Convent. Ticin.*, ii., A.D. 855, c. 11; Pertz, i., p. 432.

between churches to which tithes were paid and those to which they were not paid came to be even more important than the distinction between baptismal and non-baptismal churches, and served as the real ground-plan upon which the later parochial system was built.

It was in the course of the ninth century that this official class of country churches came to be known as "plebes," *i.e.*, peoples. The term is interesting, not only because it serves as an intermediate link between the earlier idea of a congregation and the later idea of a parish, but also because it enables us to connect the facts which relate specially to baptismal churches with another set of facts which relate to their place in the general system of ecclesiastical organisation.

The chief officer of a baptismal church was not merely a presbyter, but an *arch*presbyter. The designation was an ancient one, but in earlier times it had been applied only to an officer of the bishop's church. The archpresbyter was the head of the clergy next to the bishop. There was only one archpresbyter in a diocese, just as there was only one bishop.[1] His chief duty was to preside at the celebration of Divine service in the church when the bishop was absent. His position survives in that of the dean in the cathedral system of later times, but the name "dean," which comes from the canonical system, which will be considered in a later chapter, has almost wholly superseded the earlier name "archpresbyter." He seems to have had some control over the other presbyters, but he had no concern with the discipline of the lower clergy, which was delegated to the bishop's special assistant, the archdeacon. It was consequently natural that when separate churches came not only to exist within the bishop's jurisdiction, but also to be the chief centres of Divine worship for large areas of population, the officer who controlled such worship should bear the same designation as the similar officer in the bishop's church. We consequently find this to be the case. The Synod of Pavia in 850 enacted that there should be an arch-

---

[1] Singuli ecclesiarum episcopi, singuli archipresbyteri, singuli archidiaconi," says St. Jerome *(Epist.* 125 [95] *Ad Rusticum)*, ed. Vallars., i., 936.

presbyter for every " plebes." " And let not a bishop plead the excuse," said the Synod, " that a 'plebes' does not need an archpresbyter because he is able to govern it by himself, for however capable he may be, yet it is proper that his burdens should be eased, and that as he himself presides over the mother church, so archpresbyters should preside over country churches, that so ecclesiastical discipline may in no way falter."[1] The duties of a rural archpresbyter were extended from worship to discipline. He was to watch the clergy of the smaller churches in his district, and to report to the bishop the diligence with which they performed Divine service. The expression " the people committed to their charge," which had originally been used only in relation to bishops, came to be used in relation to archpresbyters, and with the conception which that expression implied the office of the modern parish priest may be said to have fairly begun. There were no longer merely detached congregations within the general area of a bishop's

---

[1] Hludowici II., *Conventus Ticinensis*, c. 13; Pertz, i., 399.

jurisdiction, but special areas whose inhabitants were specially entrusted to a particular presbyter, and who were to look to a particular church,[1] which was not the bishop's church, for worship, preaching, and the administration of the sacraments.

Very soon after the definite establishment of this system of baptismal churches entitled to the receipt of tithes and in the charge of arch-presbyters, we find indications of the nature of the areas of which such churches were the centres. Those areas are called by the two names " pagi " and " decaniæ." Of these the " pagus " is well known. It is the Latin equivalent of the Teutonic " gau," and consequently, like the " gau," has two senses, a wider and a narrower, the former corresponding to our English "county," and the other to our English " hundred." Just as the diocese corresponded to the former, so the area which was entrusted to an archpresbyter corresponded to the latter. In this, as in almost all similar cases, the organisation of the church followed

---

[1] "Qui ad eandem plebem aspiciunt."

the lines of the civil organisation of the country and the age in which that organisation began. The lines were already marked out, and there was no need for disturbing them. They were found in time to need subdivision, but it was only in rare cases that they were found to require rearrangement. The other word, " decania," is one of the most difficult of all the terms which are used in connection with either the civil or the ecclesiastical arrangements of the early Middle Ages. Into the complicated questions to which it gives rise it is impossible to enter here. But that it was used of the area of the jurisdiction of the original archpresbyters is one of the certain facts about it; and in time, though probably not in the first instance, archpresbyters themselves were called " decani " in the country, as they came also to be called in the bishops' churches.

The original parish in the modern sense is the rural deanery, which was at first not an aggregation of several parishes, but a single area with a single head, though comprising several churches and several clerks. The arrangements of the city church thus became the type for country districts. The archpresbyter or "dean" of the city church was reproduced in the archpresbyter of the country, or "rural dean." The one was the foremost of the clergy of the city, the other of the clergy of a district. The main point of difference was that in the city church the bishop was always present ; in the baptismal churches of the country he was present only once a year. The functions of the archpresbyter, which in the bishop's church were exercised in visible subordination to the bishop, were in country churches exercised only in theoretical subordination to him. Subject to occasional interference, and subject also in the last resort, though only in aggravated cases, and not without the right of an appeal, to expulsion from the Church, the archpresbyter of a hundred or deanery became more and more the real head of the local organisation ; and by degrees the term "parish" was transferred from the sphere of the jurisdiction of a bishop to that of the jurisdiction of an archpresbyter.

The formation of parishes less in area than the rural deanery must probably be traced to the growth of new churches which came gradually to claim the tithes of the district which immediately surrounded them. There are many enactments in regard to such churches, and it is clear from the fact that such enactments are often contradictory that there were many struggles before the smaller areas finally asserted their independence. It was at first stringently laid down that existing churches were not to be deprived of their tithes in order to provide for new churches; and the churches which first made good their claim were churches in new districts which were either newly converted to the faith or newly brought into the network of organisation. There were large outlying areas which were gradually reclaimed. There were also areas which had had a civil organisation, but which had never had a baptismal church. The result was that although in the districts which were thoroughly christianised the limits of the parish were those of the hundred, and the baptismal church was the one tithe-receiving church in the deanery, the arrangements of new districts were of a looser kind, and we find enactments to the effect that every church should settle for itself a boundary within which it might claim tithes from the farms. This arrangement gradually led to the recognition of the right of every church which was consecrated and endowed to receive tithes from the land which immediately surrounded it. Far on into the Middle Ages there were still considerable areas of unsettled or common land which were outside all ecclesiastical jurisdiction; and in our own country the final parcelling out of the whole area into defined parochial districts was probably not effected until the era of the poor-laws. But wherever a church had by endowment become a "benefice," it became also a unit of ecclesiastical jurisdiction. The original parish priest, that is the modern rural dean, exercised a certain modified and deputed control over all the clergy as well as over all the people within his deanery. But his real power and his original status tended more and more to fade into the background. His office ceased to be attached to a particular church, and might be held by any of the presbyters within the district; and though the archpresbyter held his own as against the archdeacon in the cathedral, the original relation was reversed in the rest of the diocese, and the once subordinate archdeacon became the ecclesiastical superior of the rural dean.

In this way the parish became a prominent element in the later organisation of Christianity. The territorial idea completely ousted the original idea of a community or congregation. The members of the Church were not free to worship where they pleased, or to associate for religious purposes with whom they would The framework was prepared for them in the parochial system. They were part of the flock not merely of one bishop, but of one presbyter. They were committed to his charge, and to no other could they properly look for teaching, for consolation, or for the sacraments.

Whether it is the ultimate form which the local organisation of Christianity is destined to take, or whether there may be a new form evolved out of the altered conditions of modern life ; whether it is as good for newly converted countries as it was for Europe in the Middle Ages ; or whether India, and Africa, and China might not be left to work out their own modes of Christian association, are questions which are easier to suggest than to answer, but which cannot help forcing themselves upon our attention as we see from what complicated elements and by how tortuous a process the modern parish came into being.

*TITHES AND THEIR DISTRIBUTION.*

## VI.

### TITHES AND THEIR DISTRIBUTION.

NO institution of the Middle Ages has given rise to more mistakes than the institution of tithes. Inasmuch as under the Mosaic dispensation tithes were of Divine appointment, the continuity of that appointment in the Christian dispensation has been frequently taken for granted; and inasmuch as tithes are now a main support of the clergy, and, so far as they are in the hands of the Church at all, are devoted to their exclusive use, there has been a constant tendency to assume that the clergy have an inherent and exclusive right to them.

The subject is not without important practical bearings at the present time; and it is therefore desirable, in giving a brief account of the history of tithes in the Christian Church, and of their apportionment, to add some of the historical references which place the facts beyond dispute.

1. The evidence against the view that tithes have had a continuous and general existence in the Christian Church is negative, but at the same time conclusive. It is that for the first seven centuries they are hardly ever mentioned. The regulations of councils, which touch every point of the existing ecclesiastical system, almost wholly ignore them. There are no civil enactments concerning them. In the great mass of existing deeds of donation, and of the draft forms which seem to cover the whole relations of the Church to property, they have no place. In the long lists of offences against ecclesiastical usage and discipline there is not one which concerns them. It is inconceivable that if during all that time tithes had been generally paid, or their obligation generally recognised, they should have left no contemporary trace.

Tithes as a Christian institution date, in fact, from the eighth century. They are one of the results of the great Carlovingian reformation. They are not strictly ecclesiastical in their origin, but came to the Church from the State. They were a rent paid for the leasing of church lands. Such a leasing was sometimes voluntary and sometimes compulsory. It was sometimes voluntary, as is shown by the large number of leases and draft forms of lease which remain; and it is certain that in a large proportion of cases churches gained by being relieved from the obligation to cultivate their property. It was sometimes compulsory, for, on the one hand, the State suffered from the fact that a large proportion of its territory enjoyed ecclesiastical immunities, and, on the other hand, there was a supreme necessity of finding some means of livelihood for the soldiers of the great armies which had held Europe against the Saracens. The tenth or tithe of the produce was a traditional and customary rent for lands so leased. No exception appears to have been taken at the time either to the fact of leasing or to the amount of the rent. But the amount of the rent, and the fact that it was paid to the Church, gradually created a new conception of its nature. It was identified with the Levitical tithe. But even then it was hardly considered to be of general obligation. When a race was newly conquered and compulsorily converted, an attempt was made to enforce it upon them; but it is a significant fact that Alcuin, in writing to Charlemagne to remonstrate with him for thus making Christianity a heavy burden to the Saxons, says that even those who had been born and educated in the Christian faith scarcely consented to pay tithes of their substance. The absence of all attempt to enjoin the payment of tithes in the pseudo-Isidorian Decretals is even more significant as an evidence against the general obligation of such a payment than the similar absence in earlier enactments. For those Decretals passed the whole Church system under review, and left nothing unsaid which could support the ecclesiastical power by any show of supposed ancient authority. They are an especial witness to the enormous extent to which the analogy between the Mosaic and the Christian dispensations had come to be pressed. And yet tithes are wholly absent from them. It would be impossible to find a stronger proof that at that time tithes were regarded as a legitimate rent for the use of church lands, and nothing more. It is in the period immediately succeeding the Decretals, that is about the beginning of the second half of the ninth century, that tithes begin to take a larger place in ecclesiastical literature. The turning-point may be said to be marked by a decree of the Council of Valence in 855, which, though of only local authority, indicates a current drift of opinion. The decree deals with payment of tithes as rent, about which some of the lessees of church lands appear to have been slack, and then urges their general payment by all Christians : " With respect to the properties and farms which were once offered by the faithful to the ownership of the Church, but are now subject to the power of laymen, . . . it is resolved that ninths and tenths be faithfully paid to the churches from which they have been withdrawn ; nay, moreover, let all the faithful most readily offer to God their tithes of all that they possess." Whether they were generally paid in our own country at an earlier period cannot be positively said. They are first mentioned in the Legatine Synods of 787, but the authority of a document which, though printed by honest editors (the Magdeburg Centuriators), has entirely disappeared, and cannot now be tested, is hardly sufficient of itself to prove the prevalence of a usage. The earliest certain mention of them is in the same year as the Council of Valence, which has been quoted above, under Ethelwulf, the king of Wessex; but Bishop Stubbs and Mr. Haddan, in editing the documents of that year, though they show a strong desire to make out a case for the early origin of tithes, are only able to say that "the bearing of the whole discussion on the subject of tithe appears to be merely that Ethelwulf used the tenth as a convenient measure for ecclesiastical and other benefactions, and that this testifies to an established, or at least a growing, recognition of the tithe as the clerical portion. The measure, whatever its character, affected Wessex only."[1] Within a century afterwards, that is about a century before the Norman Conquest, there is little doubt that the payment of tithes tended to become general both on the continent of Europe and in England. The analogy of the Old

---

[1] Haddan and Stubbs' *Councils and Ecclesiastical Documents*, vol. iii., p. 637.

Testament was pressed hard upon a generation which was ready to accept it, and a tenth became the ordinary measure of a Christian's offerings to God. The mass of the faithful were probably the more ready to acquiesce in the injunctions of their ministers to do as Abraham had done because thereby a limit was set on a liberality which had become too free-handed, and the payment of tithes, so far from being regarded in its modern aspect of a needless excess, was in many cases thankfully accepted as a reasonable mean.

But both throughout the Middle Ages and until the present time tithes have preserved at least one indelible mark of their origin. Being originally a rent, and sometimes a rent for land of which the State had enforced the leasing, they shared with all other kinds of rent the nature of a contract. They were consequently a payment which the State could properly enforce. From time to time indeed, and under exceptional circumstances, the secular law has lent its aid to the enforcing of other claims of the Church against property. But its enforcement of the payment of tithes has been constant.

Charles the Great wrote a letter of vigorous indignation to the soldiers who had received church lands, but declined to pay the stipulated rent for them; and the repeated enactments of his successors show that they were sufficiently alive to the benefits which the leasing of such lands brought to the community to enforce with uniform regularity the contracts which such leasing involved. Nor was there any variation in this action of the State when tithes gradually changed their character of a rent and became the customary measure of what once had been free-will offerings. In the course of the tenth century it becomes difficult to distinguish the one class of tithes from the other. There was no sharp line of separation between them, and the enforcement by law, which had properly belonged to the one, came to belong also to the other; hence throughout the Middle Ages and to the present day tithes have been a legal charge upon property, and not the least of the bonds which in most Christian countries have bound the Church to the State.

2. All offerings to the Church were originally in the disposition of the bishop, who was bound

to dispense them to all who were on the list of the needy, whether they were clergy, widows, strangers, or poor. The earliest general rule is that of the Council of Antioch in 341 (c. 25), which is a general regulation for all Church property. The earliest Eastern rule which specially mentions tithes is in the seventh book of the *Apostolical Constitutions* (c. 30), which expands a passage of the *Teaching of the Twelve Apostles*. It is as follows : " All *firstfruits* of the produce of the winepress and threshing-floor, of oxen and sheep, thou shalt give to the priests ; all *tithes* thou shalt give to the orphan and the widow, to the poor and the stranger." In the West the first mention of tithes is much later, and it will be found that when they are mentioned the distribution of them was governed by the same rule as that of other offerings to the Church.

Since the point is one of present interest, and also since the facts which bear upon it, though beyond dispute, have been ignored in some recent discussions, it will be convenient to state the more important of those facts in chronological order.

The earliest regulation is that of Pope Simplicius in 475.[1] It rules that of all the revenues of the Church and offerings of the faithful, one fourth is to go to the bishop; one fourth is to be divided among the clergy according to their several deserts; two fourths are to go to the fabrics of the churches, and to the maintenance of strangers and the poor. The regulation was recognised in later times by being incorporated in the body of Canon Law (c. 28, C. XII., qu. ii.).

The next regulation is that of Pope Gelasius in 494,[2] which gives the same rule as the preceding. Pope Gregory I.[3] finds fault with the practice which had grown up in Sicily of confining the division into four parts to the old revenues of churches, and requires that it shall be extended to newly acquired property. The letter of the same pope to Augustine of Canter-

---

[1] Jaffé, *Regesta Pontificum Romanorum*, No. 570; Thiel, *Epistolæ Romanorum Pontificum Genuinæ*, i., 175.

[2] Jaffé, No. 636; Thiel, i., 360; and in all collections of papal decretals, *e.g.*, in Dionysius Exiguus ap. Voellus et Justellus, i., 239; in the Canon Law, c. 27, C. XII., qu. ii.

[3] Jaffé, No. 1282; S. Greg. M. *Epist.* iii., 11; in the Canon Law, c. 29, C. XII., qu. ii.

bury[1] lays down the same quadripartite division, but its genuineness has been questioned.

These papal regulations were incorporated in the ordinary form of instructions which were given to a newly ordained bishop and announced to the clergy and people of his diocese;[2] hence they are found in the letter in which Pope Gregory II. in 722 commended Boniface to the clergy and people of Germany.[3]

So far there had been no special mention of tithes in these regulations, because tithes, except possibly in exceptional cases, did not exist. But about the same time that tithes are otherwise mentioned the quadripartite division is applied to them also. The first special mention of them is in a letter of Pope Zachary in 748,[4] which says: "The distribution of the tithes of the faithful which are offered in churches should not be in the power of him who offers them, for the regulations of the holy fathers say

---

[1] Jaffé, No. 1843; Bede, *H. E.*, i., 27.
[2] "Synodale quod accipit Episcopus;" in the *Liber Diurnus*, ed. de Rozière, p. 23.
[3] Jaffé, No. 2161; St. Bonifat., *Epist.* 19.
[4] Jaffé, No. 2288; St. Bonifat., *Epist.* 68.

that the bishop ought to divide them into four portions."

The earliest civil enactment on the subject is probably a law which Charlemagne made for Bavaria in 799,[1] which expressly quotes, and re-enacts in regard to tithes, the regulation of Pope Gelasius which has been given above.

From that time onwards regulations to the same effect were constant ; they required repetition, not only because different countries required separate enactments, but also because the growing claims of parish churches required some modifications of the rights of bishops. Hence the division came sometimes to be into three parts rather than four, the bishop's part being omitted. Among such regulations are the following:—

In the Council or Parliament of Aachen in 801, the clergy themselves proposed that in order to make sure of the distribution of the tithes being made in accordance with church rule, it should be made before witnesses, the first part for the decoration of the church, the

---

[1] Capit. Rhispacensia et Frisingensia, c. 13, in Pertz., i, 78, Boretius, p. 228.

second for the use of the poor and strangers, the third for the clergy themselves.[1]

In the Council of Tours in 813, it was enacted that the tithes of parish churches should be distributed by the parish presbyters, with the cognisance of the bishop, for the use of the Church and the poor.[2]

In the Council of Aachen in 817, the rule was slightly varied to the effect that in the richer churches two thirds of all Church revenues should be for the poor, one third for the clergy and monks, and that in the poorer churches they should be equally divided between the clergy and the poor.[3]

In the Council of Paris in 829, it was enacted that although the bishop was entitled to the fourth part of the tithes and other revenues of parish, as well as of other, churches, yet if he had a sufficient income from his own church, he should leave the part which was due to him from parish churches for the use of those churches and of the poor.

---

[1] Capit. Aquisgran., c. 7, Pertz, i., 87, Boretius, p. 105.
[2] 3 Conc. Turon., c. 16.
[3] Capit. Aquisgran., c. 4, Pertz, i., 206, Boretius, p. 276.

The Council of Mainz in 847 enacted that the tithes which were given to parish churches should, with the cognisance of the bishop, be carefully dispensed by the presbyters for the use of those churches and of the poor; and it went on to state the ordinary rule of quadripartite division.[1]

These regulations, which are contemporary with, and sometimes immediately added to, the original statements of the obligation of tithes, show beyond question that tithes were destined not only for the clergy, but also for the poor.

It would be improbable, even if no positive evidence on the point existed, that our own country, which followed closely in most other respects the movements and practices of the Churches of the Continent, should have differed from them in respect of the apportionment of tithes. But the positive evidence is clear. The authority of the enactments may be disputable, but they are at least witnesses to a current belief or tendency; and it can hardly be denied that whatever evidence exists in our own country

---

[1] 1 Conc. Mogunt., c. 10.

for the payment of tithes at all in pre-Norman times exists also for their appropriation, not to the clergy only, but also to the poor.

The ecclesiastical evidence is the following :—

"Let the tribute of the Church be according to the custom of the province, that is, let not the poor suffer violent wrong in respect of tithes or in any other respects. It is not lawful to give tithes except to the poor and to strangers.[1]

"The holy fathers appointed also that men pay their tithes into God's Church. And let the priest go thither and divide them into three: one part for repair of the church, and the second for the poor, the third for God's servants who attend the church."[2]

The definite civil enactment on the subject is in the "Laws of King Ethelred":—

"And respecting tithes: the King and his witan have chosen and decreed, as is just, that one third part of the tithe which belongs to the

---

[1] Capitula Theodori, in B. Thorpe, *Ancient Laws and Institutes of England*, vol ii., p. 65.

[2] *Canons of Ælfric*, in B. Thorpe, *ibid.*, vol. ii., p. 353.

Church go to the reparation of the church, and a second part to the servants of God, the third to God's poor and to needy ones in thraldom."[1]

It is true that there are civil enactments of a later date in which the division of tithes is not mentioned; and from the absence of such a mention, it has been inferred that the claim of the poor to a share in the tithes either never was recognised or has now ceased to exist. But the defence of tithes must proceed upon one or other of two lines of argument which cannot be fused together. They must either be defended as a payment to which, by virtue of civil enactments, the Church has a civil right; in this ase, he claim of the poor to a share in them may be denied, but at the same time the right of the State to pass new regulations respecting them cannot be questioned. Or they must be defended as an ancient right of the Church, resting on Divine law, and independent of, though recognised by, the State; in this case, the claim of the poor to the share in them

---

[1] *Ethelred's Laws*, 9, 6, in B. Thorpe, *Ancient Laws and Institutes of England*, vol. i., p. 343.

which the Western Churches always recognised, whenever in early times they legislated on tithes at all, can hardly be questioned. The Divine obligation to pay tithes, and the Divine right of the poor to a share in them, stand or fall together; and the emphatic words of one of the greatest ecclesiastics of the early Gallican Church, in one of the few patristic homilies which deal with tithes at all, may well be borne in mind in modern discussions:—

"Tithes are required as a due, and he who refuses to pay them has invaded other people's property. A man who does not pay his tithes will appear before the tribunal of the Eternal Judge charged with the murder of all the poor who have died of hunger in the place in which he lives, since he has kept back for his own uses the substance which God has assigned to the poor." [1]

---

[1] S. Cæsar. Arelat., *Homilia XVI.*, in Migne, *Patrologia Latina*, vol. lxvii., p. 1079; also printed as Hom. XLI. in De La Bigne, *Maxima Bibliotheca Veterum Patrum*, tom. viii., p. 858. The homily is one of those which were in such repute as to be ascribed to St. Augustine, and it is printed in that Father's works, *e.g.*, in the Benedictine Edition, tom. v., Appendix, *Sermo* CCLXXVII., p. 461.

*THE METROPOLITAN.*

## VII.

### *THE METROPOLITAN.*

IN the course of the second century of the Christian era the officers of neighbouring Christian communities began to meet together in conference. There were many points upon which unity of action and unity of discipline were desirable, and the officers met together to frame common rules. At first such conferences were held irregularly. There was no stated time or occasion for them. There was no fixed president. There was no limitation of the area from which their members were drawn. Nor did they easily take a more definite form. The Greek historians, who record the ecclesiastical history of the fourth century, make it clear that even then the same irregularity continued; and this is confirmed by the signatures to the acts of the conferences of the period. For example, the acts of the Council of Ancyra, which are still preserved, are signed by thirteen bishops from various provinces of both Asia Minor and Syria.

It was in the course of that same fourth century that a definite system in regard to the holding of such conferences began to grow up. The recognition of the Church by the State, and especially the recognition of the disciplinary acts of Church assemblies by the civil law, made the formation of such a system necessary; and one of the first acts of the Council of Nicæa was to give its sanction to the custom, which had already begun to prevail, of taking the territorial organisation of the empire as the basis of the territorial organisation of the Church. The empire was divided into provinces, and the Christian Churches within each province came to be regarded as forming a unity. The civil officers of the province met together every year at the chief city, under the presidency of a chief priest; henceforward, in a similar way, the officers of the churches within a province were to meet together, not once, but twice a year, and the bishop of the chief city of the province was recognised as having the priority of rank which is implied in *ex-officio* presidency. The purpose of the meetings was almost wholly disciplinary; the time had not yet passed when membership of a Christian Church was held to be incompatible with moral laxity of life, and expulsions from Church membership were frequent. But in order to check unjust expulsions, and also in order to secure that expulsion by one Church should be respected by other Churches, the half-yearly meeting of bishops was constituted as a court of appeal and review. The reason for emphasising the position of the bishop of the chief city of a province was in like manner almost wholly disciplinary; it was found needful to have some check upon the free election of the chief officers of individual communities, and henceforward such elections required the ratification of the " metropolitan."

But the Nicene canons rather sketched an ideal than established a general practice. Meetings of bishops continued to be held, and to pass regulations, some of which are regarded as valid to the present day, without regard to the limits of civil provinces; in some parts of the empire, certainly in North Africa and probably elsewhere, metropolitans were not recognised ; and in the fifth century the Council of Chalcedon[1] based a new regulation upon the fact that the half-yearly meetings had ceased to be regularly held. It was not until the sixth century, and, as far as existing records enable us to judge, it was only in some parts of Western Europe, that the system attained anything like a complete development. The hierarchical organisation of Gaul preserved for modern France the framework of the Roman administration. The metropolis of every Roman province, except one or two of the less important, claimed for its bishop a rank which is still indicated by the title "archbishop," a title which, though originally indicating a higher rank than that of " metropolitan,"[2] came practically to supersede it. These Western metropolitans, like those who had been recognised by the Eastern canons, claimed

---

[1] c. 19.
[2] Isid. Hispal., *Etym.*, 7, 12, adopted by Gratian, *Dist.*, xxi. c. 1.

a veto upon the appointment of bishops within their province,[1] and they had the right of summoning the other bishops of the province to synods.[2] In other respects their rights were only those of presidents; they acted with their colleagues in the provincial synods. For example, in disputes between bishops, and in appeals from a bishop's sentence, and in a dispute between a metropolitan and one of his colleagues, it was expressly enacted that the synod of his colleagues should decide.[3]

But with the growing interference of the Merovingian kings in ecclesiastical affairs, and the increasing decay of religious life which marked the end of the seventh and the first part of the eighth century, the whole system, both of metropolitans and of provincial synods, tended to pass away in Gaul, and the whirl-

---

[1] *E.g.*, at the second Council of Arles, in 452, c. 5 and 6; at the first Council of Clermont, in 535, c. 2; at the third Council of Orleans, in 538, c. 3; at the Council of Paris, in 557, c. 8.

[2] *E.g.*, at the Council of Agde in 506, c. 35; at the second Council of Orleans, in 533, c. 1.

[3] So in the fifth Council of Orleans, 549, c. 17; and in the second Council of Clermont, in the same year, c. 16.

wind of Arab conquests swept it away in Spain. There was a growing independence on the part of diocesan bishops, and consequently a growing disintegration of the Church as a whole. For although in primitive times every Christian community was independent of every other, and every Christian bishop was regarded as having received his commission direct from the Chief Shepherd,[1] the revival of this primitive status was likely to be disastrous in the altered circumstances of the ninth century. Faith and morals were alike in danger. The churches were filled with merely nominal Christians; the bishoprics were in many cases held by court nominees, and regarded chiefly as offices of emolument. It was supremely necessary not only to strengthen the hold of the local authority of the bishop over the individual communities, but also to find some means of exercising control over bishops. Consequently

---

[1] The words of the most powerful of early defenders of Catholic unity are conclusive as to the early conception of the independence of bishops: "Cum . . . singulis pastoribus portio gregis sit adscripta quam regat unusquisque et gubernet, *rationem actus sui Domino redditurus.*"—S. Cyprian, *Epist.* 59 (55) c. 14: cf. *Epist.* 55 (51) c. 21.

when Carlmann and Pippin, at the suggestion of Boniface, and supported by the influence of Rome, undertook the reform of the Churches of the Frankish domain, they wisely enacted not only that presbyters should, with certain limitations, be subject to their bishops, but also that bishops should be subject to provincial councils and metropolitans.

The revived system seems to have been tried, in the first instance, as an experiment and on a partial scale. It is not certain whether one or three metropolitans were at first appointed, but it is clear that even if three were appointed, they did not exhaust the area of the Frankish domain. The development of the system was due to Charles the Great. The enactments which he made in regard to it were repeated and explicit. The metropolitan came to have the ordinary designation of "archbishop." The other bishops came to be less frequently spoken of as his "comprovincials," and to be more commonly designated by the new word "suffragans."[1] The jurisdiction of the metro-

---

[1] The first instance in which I have found this designation

politan was no doubt intended to be not personal or arbitrary, but exercised, as in earlier times, in the common assembly of the bishops ; and both ordinary bishops and metropolitans were subject to the superior jurisdiction of the emperor. The leading enactment on the subject, which is the more interesting because the principle on which it proceeds survives in our own ecclesiastical procedure to the present day, is known as the Capitulary of Frankfort, A.D. 794.[1] It is as follows :—

"It is enacted by our lord the King and the holy synod that bishops shall exercise jurisdiction in their dioceses. If any abbot, presbyter, deacon, archdeacon, monk, or other clerk, or, indeed, any one else in the diocese, does not obey the person of his bishop, they shall come to his metropolitan, and he shall judge the cause together with his suffragans. Our counts" ("comites"—*i.e.*, the civil judges and adminis-

---

is in the Capitulary of A.D. 779, printed in Pertz, M G H, *Legum*, vol. i., p. 36, and in Boretius, M G H, *Legum*, p. 46. It next occurs in the Admonition of A.D. 789, Pertz, *l.c.*, p. 55 ; in the letter of Charles to the Bishop of Treves, A.D. 809-12, printed in Jaffé, *Monumenta Carolina*, p. 409.

[1] Printed in Pertz, *l.c.*, p. 72 ; Boretius, p. 73.

trators) " shall also come to the court of the bishops. And if there be anything which the metropolitan bishop cannot set right, then let accusers and accused both come with a letter from the metropolitan, that we" (*i.e.*, the Emperor) " may know the truth of the matter."

The position of the metropolitans was further strengthened by their frequent employment as imperial commissioners. They were sent, so to speak, " on circuit," not only to see that justice was done, but also to find out whether bishops and other officers did their duty. The fact that not only metropolitans were thus sent, but also civil officers, emphasised the fact that the new functions of metropolitans were derived not from an ecclesiastical, but from a civil source. The system, viewed merely as a piece of administrative machinery, was in theory almost perfect. On the one hand, the parish clergy had to report themselves every year, or twice a year, to their bishop, and the bishops to their metropolitan. On the other hand, there were periodical inquiries by special commissioners in each locality as to the manner in which both parish priests and bishops fulfilled their offices. The instructions given to such commissioners show the thoroughness with which the inquiry was conducted. The following is one of several examples :—

"We will that they shall diligently inquire, first, about bishops, how they fulfil their ministry, and what is their conversation, and how they order the churches and clergy committed to their charge, and what class of things they chiefly affect, that is to say, whether it be spiritual or secular; secondly, of what kind are the helpers of their ministry, that is, the archdeacons, presbyters, and others, in their several parishes, what zeal they have in doctrine, and what report they really have among the people, . . . whether the bishops in making their visitations are burdensome to the smaller parishes and oppressive to the people, and whether undue claims are made by them or their attendants upon the parish priests." [1]

It is obvious that the position of the suffragan bishops, under so strict a system of subordina-

---

[1] *Capit. Aquisgran.*, A.D. 828, in Pertz, *l.c.*, p. 329.

tion and inquiry, tended to become onerous, the more so because of the strong contrast which it presented to the preceding laxity. It is also obvious that the system was one which, resting as it did rather upon imperial than upon ecclesiastical enactments, was not in favour with those who asserted and strongly maintained the independence of the Church. The records of the period also make it clear that some metropolitans pressed their personal authority. Provincial synods again ceased to be held. The support which the State gave to those who had been in most instances its nominees compensated for the absence of ecclesiastical precedents for their action, and there was probably for a time a real danger lest the administration of the Churches of the West should be simply a branch of the ordinary administration of the empire.

But the re-establishment of metropolitans, which had been so consonant to the general policy of Charles the Great, and which had been thus thoroughly incorporated into the imperial system, had been only part of the original plan of Boniface. It is clear from his letters that just as bishops were to be subordinated to metropolitans, so metropolitans themselves were to be subordinated to the see of Rome. In a letter in reference to one of the synods which he held, Boniface describes this gradation of authority in express terms. After saying that the synod had resolved that metropolitans should obtain their " pallia," the symbols of their authority, from Rome, and should endeavour "in all things to follow the precepts of St. Peter, that we may be numbered among the sheep committed to his charge," he goes on to describe his own bond of obedience to the Roman see ; and he adds, "So, if I be not mistaken, all bishops ought to make known to their metropolitan, and the metropolitan to the Roman pontiff, whatever they themselves cannot do in the way of correcting their flocks ; and so will they be guiltless of the blood of lost souls."[1]

This idea that the metropolitans were not the supreme heads of the Churches in their respective provinces, but only intermediate between

---

[1] S. Bonifat., *Epist.* 70, in Jaffé, *Monumenta Moguntina*, p. 202.

bishops and the Roman see, worked silently but powerfully through all the Carlovingian period; and when, on the one hand, the bishops felt the yoke of the metropolitans to be too heavy, and, on the other hand, the emperors had become too weak to resist a strongly asserted papal claim, the subordination which Boniface had foreshadowed began to be a real fact. The bishops felt that their only immediate chance of freedom from the oppression of their local rulers was in the support which they might derive from the Roman pontiffs; and it was in the interests of the bishops that a series of documents was composed which has largely affected all subsequent Church history. Into the existing collections of the decrees of councils and the letters of popes were interwoven documents of the same kind, to the uncritical eye not distinguishable from them, which almost all tended in the direction of asserting the subordination of metropolitans to higher powers. The interpolated collection passed for a genuine one. It was adopted by the popes, probably in the first instance without suspicion; and though now commonly called even by papal advocates "the *False* Decretals," it was for many centuries an unquestioned body of ecclesiastical law.[1]

It was thus as a reaction against the excessive powers with which the policy of the Carlovingians had invested metropolitans that the great revolution was brought about which transformed the independent Churches of the West into vassals of the Roman see. Metropolitans continued to exist, but they existed only as intermediaries between the pope and the ordinary bishops. The ampler powers which they had come to exercise partly in their own interest and partly in the interest of the emperor were continued to them in the interest of the pope. They were convenient local depositaries of the powers which were claimed by the successors of St. Peter. Though constantly superseded and set aside by legates *a latere*, and though no longer able, even in a provincial synod, to pronounce a definitive sentence against an offending colleague, they still possessed large powers of administration. To their one original right

---

[1] The great edition of Hinschius (*Decretales pseudo-Isidorianæ*, Berlin, 1870) by the use of different type for the interpolated portions has made the drift of those portions obvious to any student who can construe ecclesiastical Latin.

of approving or disapproving of the election of a bishop by a Church, they added the right of visitation, of supersession, and of the administration of a vacant see.

If it be admitted that the primitive freedom of local Churches was no longer either possible or desirable, it may be admitted also that, subject to the control of a great central authority, the powers of the mediæval metropolitan were inevitable and beneficial. But such an admission hardly touches the question of the status of metropolitans in a Reformed Church in modern times. The effect of the Reformation on metropolitans was practically to leave them all their acquired powers, and at the same time to take away the ecclesiastical check upon the exercise of those powers, and to substitute for it the check of the civil power. The contention of many estimable persons is that this form of check, against which no doubt many arguments may be urged, should be itself taken away. The effect of taking it away would be to leave metropolitans with large powers which have been mainly derived from the State, and which, so far as they have been allowed by the Church, have been allowed only with efficient safeguards against abuse, uncontrolled, and liable to the same abuses as before. A reform of the Church which consisted simply, as far as metropolitans were concerned, in the removal of a check upon the powers which the Canon Law gradually gave them, would be a new experiment in Church polity which could hardly fail to end in disaster. The whole system which the Canon Law constructed stands or falls together. If the checks upon its machinery be abandoned, the machinery itself must be abandoned also. The only safe direction which a movement for reform can take, in this as in other respects, is that of a return, with whatever modifications of detail our altered circumstances may demand, to the primitive polity, according to which each group of Churches, knit together by the spiritual bonds of Christian fellowship, managed its own affairs, exercised its own discipline, appointed its own officers, and committed to the person of a president only those administrative and executive functions which in all societies must be exercised, or at least exercised *ad interim*, by a single officer.

*NATIONAL CHURCHES.*

# VIII.

## *NATIONAL CHURCHES.*

THE formation of National Churches is an extension, though not in the original direction, of the same process which led to the institution of provincial synods. The original conceptions of Christian association were but two in number—that of the single congregation, and that of the whole aggregate of believers throughout the world. Both were designated by the same word, " Church," but the former was limited by the addition of the name of the locality,—the " Church of God which is at Corinth," or " the Church of the Thessalonians,"—while the latter was simply " the Church," or " the Church of God," or, from the second century onwards, "the General Church " ($\dot{\eta}$ καθολικὴ ἐκκλησία). In the New Testament, and for some time afterwards, the

Christian communities within a wide geographical area are spoken of, not in he singular, but in the plural : " the Churches of Judea," or " of Galatia." It was only by slow degrees that the fact of neighbourhood was conceived to give Churches a title to interfere in the concerns of another Church ; and the councils of the fourth century show that the recognition of the imperial " province " as the legitimate area of association was also slow and gradual. But that which is slowly formed is often also permanent ; this grouping of Christian communities according to the Roman provinces in which they were situated survives to the present day, and an analogous arrangement is extended to countries which, so far from having had a Roman organisation, were altogether outside the horizon of the Roman world. It was a voluntary arrangement. It was generally accepted, in the first instance, because it was found to be convenient. But it was at the time artificial. There was nothing in the nature of the Roman provincial organisation to give it a sacredness which does not attach to other organisations. A grouping of Churches according to the areas of river basins or of local dialects would have been, if less convenient, yet not less Divine. A precisely similar arrangement exists among some of the non-conforming communities of our own time and country. They form "county associations," which hold annual meetings and exercise a certain kind of supervision over individual congregations; and, although individual congregations are in most instances as free as the primitive communities were to withdraw from the association, or to refuse to submit to its decisions, they usually find it convenient to maintain the bond of connection.

But a system which is the product of considerations of expediency tends also to be modified by considerations of expediency. In certain of its features the grouping of Churches according to Roman provinces, or combinations of provinces, has been permanent; but in certain other features it has given way to a system of grouping according to political divisions, in which the organisation of the Roman empire has been superseded or ignored. Provincial Churches have been succeeded by national Churches. The ideas of grouping according to locality, and of giving to the majority a control over the individual, have remained. But the locality is conterminous with the State, and the majority which exercises control is the majority, not of the immediate neighbourhood, but of the whole political area.

The external causes of the change are to be found in the history of the Teutonic kingdoms which rose upon the ruins of the Roman Empire. The limits of those kingdoms were constantly shifting, and were determined without regard to the limits of existing dioceses or provinces. For whereas the latter had been determined, in Roman times, chiefly by the areas of settlement of the original tribes of Celts, the latter were determined by the areas of settlement or conquest of the intrusive tribes of the Teutons. Each kingdom found an ecclesiastical organisation existing, and endeavoured to incorporate it. The earlier bonds began to give way under the pressure of the new need of keeping the kingdom together. The kings gathered together the bishops and clergy within their domain, irrespective of the earlier arrangements. The bishops and clergy obeyed the king's summons without regard to the questions which have been raised in later times as to the precise nature of his authority. The type of kingly power which presented itself to their minds, and which was in entire harmony with the growing conception of the ministry as a priesthood, was that of the Old Testament. Nor was their obedience the less ready because the summons was addressed, not only to them, but also to laymen. It was as natural that the king should call together both bishops and nobles to consult for the common good as that Josiah should, in ancient days, have gathered together, not only the priests and prophets, but also "the men of Judah and the inhabitants of Jerusalem." And when assembled in such mixed meetings of clergy and laity under the king's authority, they did not attempt to draw a sharp distinction between secular and ecclesiastical affairs. Whatever affected the people at large came within the sphere of their control. Out of such meetings grew the sense of a unity which was not only political, but also ecclesiastical. The nation and the Church of the nation grew from the same roots and side by side. Each was independent of external control, but neither asserted an independence of the other.

In this general sketch of the rise of the national Churches of the West out of the assemblies which were summoned by the kings of the new Teutonic kingdoms, there are three points which it is important to note and to prove:—

(1) That these assemblies were summoned by kings, and not by bishops;

(2) That they consisted not only of clergy, but also of laity;

(3) That they exercised a control, not only over purely civil, but also over purely ecclesiastical affairs, laying down rules and deciding cases of precisely the same kind as those of the earlier ecclesiastical assemblies of Africa or Asia Minor.

(1) The first of these points is proved by the statements of the assemblies themselves. In the great majority of cases their resolutions are prefaced by a declaration that the assembly was convoked by the king's orders or with his consent. For example, if we take only those

assemblies which have sometimes been claimed as exclusively ecclesiastical, the preface of what is known as the First Council of Orleans, in 511, states that it was convoked "at the summons of the most glorious king Chlodwig;" the Second Council of Orleans, in 533, "at the bidding of the most glorious kings;" the Council of Macon in 581, "at the summons of Gunthram;" the Council of Valence in 584, "according to the order of Gunthram."[1] And if we take the assemblies which, more than any others, determined the constitution of the mediæval Churches, the form is even more explicit, for example, "I, Carlman, leader and prince of the Franks, with the counsel of the servants of God and my nobles, have assembled the bishops who are in my kingdom, together with the presbyters, as a council and synod, . . . that they may give me advice how the law of God and ecclesiastical discipline may be recovered, which in the days of past princes have fallen into ruin, and how Christian folk

---

[1] A list of such statements, which it is not necessary to multiply here, will be found in Waitz, *Deutsche Verfassungsgeschichte*, Bd. ii., abth. i., p. 201 (3$^{te}$ aufl.).

may come to the salvation of their souls and not perish deceived by false priests."[1]

(2) That the assemblies consisted, not only of clergy, but also of laity, is also proved by the statements of the assemblies themselves. A distinction of times and places must no doubt be drawn. To a certain extent, and under the rule of the Merovingians more than elsewhere, the purely ecclesiastical assemblies continued to exist, and to exercise purely ecclesiastical discipline. Their existence and their action were a necessary part of the judicial system of the time. For the Roman law, which continued to exist for the clergy, recognised the disciplinary functions of synods; and the exercise of such functions was part of the inheritance of freedom to which the clergy clung, not so much in their capacity of clerks as in their capacity of descendants of the Romans. But these purely ecclesiastical assemblies gradually lost their original importance, and at last almost entirely disappeared. They were overshadowed and thrust out of existence by the mixed

---

[1] Karlmanni Principis Capitulare, in Pertz, M. G. H., vol. i., p. 16; Boretius, i., 24.

## NATIONAL CHURCHES. 147

assemblies, which have for Englishmen a special interest, inasmuch as they were the immediate historical precursors and prototypes of our English parliaments. The enacting clauses of the decrees of these mixed assemblies tell their own tale. In the West Gothic kingdom, for example, the First Council of Toledo consisted, not only of bishops, but also of the nobles and officers of the palace ("optimates et seniores palatii"); in the Third Council of Toledo, the king expressly promulgates a canon with the consent of the chief men in the kingdom ("cum suorum optimatum illustriumque virorum consensu"); in the "tome" of the Thirteenth Council of Toledo King Erwig addresses as constituent members of the assembly, not only the bishops, but also the chief officers of his court ("universitatem paternitatis vestræ atque sublimium virorum nobilitatem qui ex aulæ regalis officio in hac synodo vobiscum consessuri prælecti sunt"). In the Frankish kingdom, though there is a controversy as to the precise character of some of the Merovingian assemblies, the statements of the assemblies after the time of Pippin are repeated and clear. The enactments of Soissons, for example, in 744, are made "with the consent of the bishops and priests and servants of God, and by the advice of the counts and nobles of the Franks;" the first edict of Charles the Great is made "on the recommendation of the Apostolic See, and by the advice of all my faithful lieges, especially the bishops and other priests;" the canons of Heristall, in 779, are made at a synodical council of "bishops, abbots, nobles, and counts." Even where other laymen are not mentioned, and may possibly not have been present, the king himself was an integral factor in the assembly. For example, in the Synod of Frankfort, in 794, " the most gracious king was himself present,"—" ipse mitissimus sancto interfuit conventui,"—and the canons were made "by our lord the king and the holy synod."[1] So it was also in our own country.

---

[1] The facts which relate to this important synod will be found in the *Annales Laureshamenses*, in Pertz, M. G. H., *Scriptorum*, i., p. 36; *Chronicon Moissacense*, *ibid.*, p. 300; *Annales Fuldenses*, *ibid.*, p. 351: and its acts in Pertz, *Legum*, i., p. 71; Boretius, i., p. 73.

## NATIONAL CHURCHES.

The *Witenagemot* was often as much ecclesiastical as civil. For example, at the meeting which is known as the Council of Bapchild, near Sittingbourne, the members are specified as Wihtred, King of Kent, Berhtwald, "Archbishop of Britain," the Bishop of Rochester, abbots, abbesses, presbyters, deacons, and king's officers.[1] The acts of the Legatine Synod of 787, whatever be their value, are subscribed not only by bishops, but also by Offa, King of the Mercians, and the "Ealdormen."[2] And lest it should be urged that this was a local usage out of harmony with the general usages of Christian Churches, it may be useful to draw special attention to the fact that, when the circumstances of the English Church were discussed in a council at Rome, in 679, it was resolved that Archbishop Theodore should assemble a "general council," or "public and œcumenical synod," whose members are described in the comprehensive terms of "universis

---

[1] "Ducibus satrapis" in the MSS. printed in Birch's *Cartularium Saxonicum*, vol. i., p. 128; "manige wise menn" in the *Anglo-Saxon Chronicle*.

[2] Haddan and Stubbs' *Councils*, etc., vol. iii., p. 460.

præsulibus, regibus, principibus, et universis fidelibus, senioribus majoribusque natu totius Saxoniæ."[1] Such meetings were in fact the ordinary assemblies which were part of the common heritage of the Teutonic races. The bishops sat in them as being among the most prominent men and competent counsellors in the kingdom.

(3) The third point, that these mixed assemblies took cognisance of ecclesiastical as well as of civil affairs, is also shown by their records. It cannot be disputed that they sometimes dealt, not only with the external affairs of the Church, but also with ritual and with doctrine; nor can it be disputed that they did not confine themselves to laying down general rules, but also sometimes acted as a supreme court, exercising what in later times would have been claimed to be purely spiritual authority. It was in one of these mixed national assemblies, that is to say, in the Third Council of Toledo, A.D. 589, that the "filioque" clause was added to the Creed of Western Christendom; and it

---

[1] Haddan and Stubbs, vol. iii., p. 134.

is not less remarkable that the recitation of the Creed in the Communion Office is a survival of an enactment which was made in that same assembly, and made, moreover, not by the ecclesiastical element in it, but by King Reccared alone.[1] In the same way the Synod of Frankfort, in 794, which has been mentioned above, took cognisance of and condemned the theory of Elipandus, Bishop of Toledo, regarding the nature of the Divine Sonship, which is commonly known as "Adoptionism;" and it is expressly recorded that the condemnation was the act of the whole assembly, not only the bishops, but also the other members. In our own country the "dooms" of Ine, which were made at a Wessex Witenagemot, about 690, relate to baptism and the observance of Sunday.[2] The laws of Edgar, of Ethelred, and of Canute, all deal with ecclesiastical as well as with secular matters. The Teutonic settlers in England, in this as in other respects,

---

[1] The documents will be found in all collections of the councils, *e.g.*, in Bruns, vol. i., p. 212.

[2] Thorpe, *Ancient Laws*, pp. 44—65; Haddan and Stubbs, vol. iii., pp. 214—218.

developed their institutions on the same general lines as the Teutonic settlers on the continent of Europe.

It was in this way, by the holding of meetings at which both the ecclesiastical and civil elements were represented, and which dealt with ecclesiastical no less than with civil questions, that there grew up the conceptions of both ecclesiastical and political unity which, more than physical force, welded together the diverse populations of what are now Spain, France, and England, each into a single whole. The older Roman arrangements lasted on, but only for limited purposes. The province was superseded by the nation in almost all respects, except that of internal discipline. The meetings of bishops in provincial councils tended to vanish under the influence of their meeting side by side with the nobles and civil officers in the more important national council. Of the ecclesiastical unit which was so formed the national council was the only representative. The Gallican Church and the English Church exist as units only so far as they are held together by this national bond. They are not mere combinations of Roman provinces, but arose out of circumstances in which the Roman provinces were ignored. The breaking of the bond which binds the national Church together would not necessarily leave the fabric of the Roman provincial organisation in possession of the ground. The question would naturally arise whether the province as a basis of ecclesiastical association was destined to be any more permanent than the nation. If Churches are to form groups, it is better, as a matter of expediency and sentiment, that they should be grouped upon a system which has a past history rather than upon one which is wholly new. But there is nothing to show that a grouping according to the lines of the Roman provinces is more in accordance with the Divine will than a grouping according to English counties. All groupings are artificial. The measure of the Divine will is the spiritual good that comes of grouping. He would be a strong Erastian who should maintain that no combination of Churches is allowable except upon the lines of the political divisions of a given time. He would be no less an Erastian who should maintain that the decisions of a group of Churches, which, being held together by the political bond, form the national Church, have a sacredness and a force which would not attach to the decision of a group which had been formed on a non-political system. The great mediæval institution of national Churches claims our respect as an instrument of spiritual good in the past, and the particular Church to which we belong claims also our allegiance as the instrument with which God has appointed us to work in the present ; but the sacredness of the institution attaches not so much to the fact of its existence as to the spirit which prompts its members, nor can it be shown that any blessing rests upon it which does not also rest upon all congregations of " two or three " who are gathered together in the name of Christ.

*THE CANONICAL RULE.*

## IX.

### *THE CANONICAL RULE.*

THE conversion of the Teutonic and Celtic races was a slower process than has sometimes been supposed. For several centuries after the adhesion of the Frankish kings to the Catholic faith, although the network of Christian organisation appeared to cover the greater part of the Frankish domain, Christianity was, in fact, only a thin veneer over the surface of a pagan society. It was the religion of the court, and of the survivors of the Roman population; but it was not the religion of the masses of the people. The Teutonic gods were openly worshipped. In some places their altars stood by the side of the Christian churches. It was thought not only that the two religions might coexist in the State, but also that the gods of their forefathers and the God of the Christians might be worshipped side by side. Even after the majority of the people began to come to Christian worship, and to receive the Christian sacraments, heathen practices lingered on a considerable scale. One of the earliest enactments of Charles the Great, for example, renewed an enactment of his uncle Carlman against "the foolish men who offered sacrifices close to churches in pagan fashion in the name of holy martyrs and confessors;"[1] and the "list of superstitions and paganisms," which was drawn up by an unknown person in the eighth century, and which still survives in a Vatican MS., is not less interesting to a student of religion than it is to a student of folk-lore.[2]

The survival of heathen practices in religion was accompanied by, and was possibly a result of, the survival of heathen practices in ordinary life. The statute-books of the Teutonic races are unimpeachable witnesses on the point. The

---

[1] Karoli M., *Capitulare Primum*, A.D. 769, c. 8; Pertz, M. G. H., *Legum*, vol. i., p. 34; Boretius, p. 45, renewing Karlmanni *Capitulare*, A.D. 742, c. 5; Pertz, p. 17; Boretius, p. 25.

[2] *Indiculus Superstitionum et Paganiarum*, in Pertz, vol. i., p. 19; Boretius, p. 222.

vice of the North, then as now, was drunkenness. The indications of grossness in common living, in respect of both drinking and eating, are almost incredible, and cannot be here detailed ; and even more repulsive are the indications of still grosser vices which accompanied it. Nor was there any powerful influence at work to counteract the current paganism. The relation of the clergy of the time to the morality of the time was not what might have been antecedently expected, or what has ordinarily prevailed. For the period was almost unique in Christian history in its complete relaxation of the bonds of ecclesiastical discipline. Wandering bishops ordained wandering clergy, and neither bishops nor clergy were easily brought to acknowledge a superior. In the century which had immediately succeeded the collapse of the Roman administration the majority of the clergy were Romans, citizens of the Roman municipalities, imbued with Roman traditions, and on a higher level of civilisation than the greater part of those to whom they ministered. In the eighth century the clergy, as is shown by their names, were mostly Teutons or Celts ;

and they do not seem to have been far removed from the ordinary level of their countrymen. Not only had the Christian ministry become a profession and means of livelihood; it had also become a lucrative profession. The great increase in the wealth of the Christian churches had fostered the growth of a class of clergy who were almost completely secularised. They hunted; they hawked; they traded; they lent money upon usury. And with the secularisation of their office came the degradation of its ideal of living. It is no doubt easy to frame an indictment against the clergy of any period, and not only against the clergy, but against any class of society, by raking together, and presenting in one view, all recorded instances of misconduct. But the inference of the low level of clerical life in the eighth century is drawn not from individual instances, but from the fact of repeated legislation. There are laws which are too explicit to refer to an imaginary state of things, and too frequently repeated to be explained by the hypothesis of a rare or transitory phenomenon, against clerks frequenting taverns, staying there until midnight, and tottering about the church from drunkenness while engaged in holy offices.[1]

Against this degradation of clerical life there came a profound and permanent reaction. That reaction came from monasticism. The first impulse was given to it by the preaching of monks, in whom we may ourselves take an especial interest, inasmuch as they belonged to a great extent to our own islands: to the monasteries of Ireland and Scotland and the south of England. The impulse which they gave was chiefly that of their own example. The influence of that example worked silently for at least a century before it showed itself in the common life of the clergy. But gradually, and side by side with the restoration of ecclesiastical discipline, which gave birth to the mediæval

---

[1] See, *e.g.*, S. Gregorii Papæ, *Excerptum de diversis criminibus et remediis eorum*, in Migne's *Patrologia Latina*, vol. lxxxix., 587—593; the Carlovingian Capitularies, for example in Pertz, M. G. H., i., 138, 139, 160, 440; the decrees of councils, for example the Third Council of Tours, A.D. 813, c. 21, the Second Council of Chalons, in the same year, c. 10, the Council of Cloveshoe, A.D. 747, c. 21; and the regulations of bishops, such as Theodulf of Orleans, Hincmar of Rheims, and others, in Mansi, *Concilia*, vol. xii., p. 283, vol. xiii., p. 993, vol. xiv., p. 393, vol. xv., pp. 475, 505.

diocese and the mediæval parish, rose the institution of semi-monastic life for the clergy, which gave birth to the mediæval cathedral. The one and the other—for the one was the complement of the other, and both were parts of a great ecclesiastical reformation — were brought about by the co-operation of Church and State, by the civil authority of the Frankish kings, and the spiritual influence of the Bishop of Rome. They agreed in fostering the policy of withdrawing the clergy from ordinary society, of setting before them the ideal which had been from time to time framed for them by general and local councils, and of imposing upon them a common rule of discipline.

This institution of the "canonical rule," or "common life," for the clergy has had such wide ramifications, and fills so large a place in modern ecclesiastical systems, that it will probably be interesting to trace its beginnings and early developments.

The first trace of it in legislation is in a decree of the Council of Vernon in 755.[1] It

---

[1] c. 11, Pertz, p. 26; Boretius, p. 35.

was there enacted that clerks should live either in a monastery under monastic order, or under the control of the bishop under "canonical" order. In a capitulary of Pippin for his kingdom of Lombardy in 782,[1] the bishop was required to compel his clergy to live under "canonical" order; and if he failed to do this, the king's officer was to decline to treat them as clerks and to put them on a level with other freemen in regard to liability to military service. That this penalty was an onerous one may be inferred from the number of persons who became clerks in order to escape it. The meaning of the term "canonical order" is more explicitly given a few years later in an enactment of Charles the Great at Aachen, which first requires presbyters and bishops to live "according to the canons," and then gives the following summary of what is required from those who live the canonical life : " Let them not be permitted to wander out of doors, but let them live under complete ward, not given to filthy lucre, not unchaste, not thieves, not murderers, not

---

[1] c. 2, Pertz, p. 42; Boretius, p. 191.

ravishers, not litigious, not passionate, not puffed up, not drunkards, but chaste in heart and body, humble, modest, sober, kind, peaceful, sons of God worthy of being promoted to holy orders, not living lives of luxury or unchastity or other kinds of iniquity in the villages or homesteads adjoining a church without control or discipline." . . .[1]

This was the first stage of legislation on the subject. It is obvious that, assuming the truth of the terrible indictment against the clergy which the last-quoted enactment implies, such legislation was needed. It is also clear, from the repetition of such enactments, and from the instructions given to imperial commissioners to see them carried out, that Charles was thoroughly in earnest in this work of ecclesiastical reform. The next stage of legislation was to provide the material conditions for living such a life. The theory was that in cities the bishop and his clergy, and in country places the chief presbyter and the younger clergy, should live together under the same roof. Where the bishop's house

---

[1] *Capitulare Aquisgranense*, A.D. 802, c. 10, 22; Pertz, pp. 92, 94; Boretius, pp. 93, 95.

was not large enough, another building was to be provided; but whether it were the bishop's house or another building, it was a "claustrum," or "cloister," a building kept under lock and key, with a common refectory and, above all, a common dormitory. In the third stage it was enacted that those who thus lived together, "according to the canons," and in a common building, should live by a common rule. Early in the history of the movement, about 760, a Frankish bishop, Chrodegang of Metz, had recast the monastic rule of St. Benedict into a form suitable for the conditions of clerical instead of monastic life. In a meeting held at Aachen in 816 or 817, Lewis the Pious adopted this rule, with some modifications and additions, and made the observance of it obligatory. In the original form of the rule the bishop and archdeacon were mentioned as the administrative officers of the clergy who thus lived together; the conception was simply that of a bishop's house, regulated by strict rules of life. In the form which was sanctioned at Aachen the bishop is relieved from the ordinary duty of seeing that the rules of life are observed, and the place of the archdeacon is supplied by the "præpositus," or provost, an officer who might, no doubt, be the archdeacon, but who had a more general name because some cloisters were detached from the bishop's house, and were consequently outside the oversight of an officer of the bishop's church. In both forms of the rule the clergy-house was to have only one door for entrance and for exit: it was to contain a dormitory, a refectory, a store-room, and other offices necessary for brethren living together in a single society; the clergy were to receive food and drink in prescribed portions; those who had no means of their own were to receive clothing as well.[1]

The succeeding Carlovingian emperors continued the policy of Charles and Lewis, and in doing so were supported by the popes. The clergy seem to have struggled against it. At Meaux and Epernay in 845 the rules of Aachen

---

[1] The canonical rule, both in the form framed by Chrodegang and in that which was authorised at Aachen, which have been not infrequently confused, has been repeatedly printed, *e.g.*, Mansi, *Concilia*, vol. xiv., pp. 153, 315; Walter, *Fontes Juris Ecclesiastici*, p. 20.

were revived with a minuteness and stringency which implies that they had been broken ; the bishops were required to provide cloisters for all their clergy; if their own houses were not large enough for the purpose, they were empowered to acquire neighbouring land, by compulsion if necessary ; if they had not funds with which to build, the emperor undertook to levy forced contributions for the purpose on the holders of Church lands. The rule became as general in Italy and England as it had become in the Frankish domain, and by the beginning of the tenth century the canonical life embraced almost all the clergy in Western Christendom.[1]

It was a great and beneficent reformation. It rescued the clergy of the West from a growing degradation. It took a deep and permanent root in Christian society, because it satisfied a great need. It gave an ideal of life which appreciably raised the standard of clerical

---

[1] The canonical life is mentioned in England as early as the Legatine Synods of 787 ; but this fact is only one of several proofs that the canons of those synods, at least in their present form, are of a later date than that to which they profess to belong. See Haddan and Stubbs' *Councils*, etc., vol. iii., p. 450.

living; and however much some of its collateral effects may be regretted, it has in itself played an important part in the development of both Christian morals and Christian theology.

Its immediate purposes were determined by the causes out of which it arose ; they were two in number, discipline and instruction.

1. The discipline mainly consisted in the obligation to eat and sleep in a common building. It thus checked on the one hand the prevalent tendency to gluttony and drunkenness, and on the other hand the tendency to immorality. The check which it imposed in this latter respect was part of the general and growing drift towards celibacy. That drift must be estimated not by its relation to the conditions of our own settled society, but by its relation to a time in which, through the clash of new forces and shifting populations, morality and civilisation were for a time unhinged. Just as in our own time it is necessary in certain cases, and among certain classes of the population, to meet a great prevalent vice by a total abstinence from intoxicating drink, so, it may at least be contended, it was necessary to meet

another great group of vices by withdrawing the clergy altogether from intercourse with female society. It is probable that this element in the idea of a canonical life was foremost in the minds of those who promoted it. The canons of which they thought were the enactments of successive councils which restricted or prohibited the marriage of the clergy; the Roman Council of 853, for example, gives as the express reason for requiring priests to live in cloisters, "that they may avoid the company of women."

The strict discipline of this common life became the stricter because it was combined with, and largely fostered, the penitential system which has since played so considerable a part in the Christian world. The habit of confessing sins became part of a fixed ecclesiastical rule. The sins which the canonical clergy confessed were mainly offences against the discipline of the common life. Lists of such offences were drawn up, and the penalty for each offence was specified. From the time of the establishment of the canonical system "penitential books" began to multiply; and there is no darker page in the history of Christianity than the state of life which they reveal. The very foulness of the sins for which they prescribe is the best justification for their existence ; for if such sins prevailed even under a system of checks and surveillance, the state of clerical morality before that system began, and which might have continued if that system had not existed, must have been inconceivably immoral. The system, which began by being one of interior discipline for clergy-houses, was gradually extended to the laity ; and the confession of sins, which had been an almost inevitable adjunct of the canonical discipline, was ultimately made a condition of admission to communion for all Christians alike. The history of the practice is of especial interest, and also of especial value, in view of its revival within our own borders in recent times.

2. The second purpose which the canonical rule was designed to serve was that of edification and instruction. The hours of the day and night were apportioned to definite occupations, chief among which were those of praying and reading. Seven times in twenty-four hours did the summons sound for prayers and for

## THE CANONICAL RULE.

the recitation of the Psalms. The "canonical hours" became a fixed institution of Christendom; and they have left their mark on the daily services of our own Church, which in their form do but perpetuate the daily services of the early mediæval clergy-houses. Every day the clergy met to celebrate the mass, and every day they also met for the reading of part of either the Bible, or the canons, or the canonical rule, or " treatises and homilies which should edify the hearers."[1] It is probable that the later name for this daily meeting, and afterwards also for the persons who so met together, was derived from the phrase by which it is designated in Chrodegang's rule, viz., " ad capitulum," *i.e.*, to hear a " chapter " read. In this way the prevalent ignorance of the clergy was lessened. Learning began to form a necessary ingredient in their life, and the mere fact of their seclusion from other occupations tended to lift them above the level of the time at which a bishop had diligently to inquire whether a presbyter knew the Creed.

[1] Chrodegangi *Regula*, c. 8; and Alcuini, *Epist.* 50, in Haddan and Stubbs' *Councils*, vol. iii., p. 502.

One effect of this element in the canonical rule is of especial interest. It was the duty of the elder clerks to see that the younger were taught. In country clergy-houses the duty devolved upon the presiding presbyter, or parish priest; in city clergy-houses there came to be a special officer, the "scholasticus," who, from the fact that he was also the secretary of the canonical clergy, was also known, especially in England, as the "cancellarius," or chancellor. In some cases, he came in course of time to be detached from the clergy-house altogether; and in some such cases, others besides the young clerks of the clergy-house clustered round him for instruction. It is possible that the dignified position of the Chancellor of the University of Oxford only is the historical continuation of that of the schoolmaster and secretary of the canons of St. Frideswide.

*THE CATHEDRAL CHAPTER.*

## X.

### *THE CATHEDRAL CHAPTER.*

THE earliest regulations respecting the canonical life appear to have contemplated only the case of the clergy of a city living together in the bishop's house. Consequently in the rule of Chrodegang the bishop was the actual, as well as the nominal, head of the clergy to whom the rule applied. He had the chief seat at the chief table. He assigned to the several clerks their several duties. He distributed the stipends and the clothes. He was the disciplinary officer, not by way of appeal, but in the first instance. Under him, following the traditional lines, the archdeacon was the chief officer of the community. The gradations of rank and function which existed in the church in respect of the discipline of Divine service existed also in the adjoining clergy-house in respect of the discipline of daily life.

But subsequent regulations contemplate the case of other clergy-houses, besides that which was attached to the bishop's church. Consequently in the rule which was authorised at Aachen, and by which the subsequent communities were governed, the bishop is the nominal rather than the actual head ; the actual head is the "præpositus" or "provost;" and the clergy, who lived together in their several communities, began to have an internal organisation of their own, apart from the general organisation of the whole Christian community.

It is not proposed in these pages to enter into the history of the other communities which the rule of Aachen covered, and which have generally been known as collegiate churches; but confining our view to the community of the clergy of the bishop's church, it is proposed to show by the operation of what causes that community came to have the important share in ecclesiastical administration which belongs to the mediæval and modern "cathedral chapter." The present chapter will deal with the growth of (1) its independence and (2) its separate internal organisation ; the following chapter with its status in relation to the diocese.

I. The primary cause of the independence of the cathedral chapter is to be found in that which is the motive cause of most constitutional changes, both within the church and without it : the " love of money." The clergy who lived in the bishop's house, and under a common rule of life, differed from monks in respect chiefly of not being bound, as monks were, by the obligation of perpetual poverty. They could acquire property. They could amass savings. They had thus a keener interest than monks had in their several shares in the funds of the church. The ancient theory that those funds were at the disposal of the bishop had long been modified by the rule that he should divide them into three or four equal portions, of which one portion was for the clergy and one for the poor. But with the enormous increase in the funds of the church, and with the absence of a sufficient check upon the action of bishops, the rule had come to be frequently set aside. The avarice of bishops came to be a constant subject of complaint. The shares both of the clergy and of the poor were inadequate and irregular. It became neccessary to withdraw some of the sources of income from the bishop's control, and one of the first effects of the new power which came to the city clergy from their living in common was the assignment of the lands of the church and of the tithes of certain districts to separate purposes, one portion to the bishop and one to the clergy.[1] The same course was soon adopted in respect of the portion of the poor ; and before long there were three separate funds and three sets of estates, one belonging to the bishop, a second to the clergy, a third to the sick, the strangers, and the poor. The bishop's house, which had formerly been also a clergy-house and a " hospitium " or house for strangers, became simply the bishop's residence, and separate from it, though side by side with it,

---

[1] A good early instance of this partition of revenues between a bishop and his clergy is that of Paris; the deed, which bears the date 829, still exists, and is printed by Guérard, *Cartulaire de l'Eglise Notre Dame de Paris*, pp. lxii., 321.

were the "cloister" of the canons and the "hospital" for the needy.

The first effect of this assignment of particular estates to the body of clergy, or " canons," who were living together, was to give to that body a corporate character, an independence which it had not before possessed in respect of the bishop, and a status distinct from that of the other clergy of the diocese.

A second result was to limit the number of persons who could be placed upon the list of cathedral clergy. Hitherto the discretion of the bishop had been unlimited. The persons whom he ordained took their place, as of course, on the list, and received their share of the offerings. But though this discretion continued to be unlimited in respect of country clergy, the number of the cathedral clergy usually came to be fixed ; the canons declined to permit an increase in their number, and a consequent diminution of their individual shares in the common fund, without their consent.[1]

---

[1] A good early instance of this is in the regulation of the Synod of Cologne in 873 (Mansi, *Concilia*, vol. xvii., 275) confirming the partition of the revenues which had been made six years previously.

A third result was to subdivide the whole endowment thus given over to the cathedral clergy, and to assign definite sources of income to each individual member of it. It naturally and rapidly followed that the canon to whom lands or tithes were assigned for his support claimed a right of property in them, and that a canonry, from having been merely a claim to a share in a common meal and a common lodging, became a legal benefice, sometimes with large emoluments, and always with the rights of a freehold.

A fourth result was that canonries, having become places of both dignity and emolument, were sought after as such by persons who had no proper claim to them. So far from being means of providing for the material needs of the clergy of a cathedral or parish church, they came to be sometimes held by laymen, either as sources of income, or as offices of honour. The Roman emperor was a canon of St. Peter's and St. John Lateran at Rome, of Utrecht, Cologne, and Aix-la-Chapelle; the Pope himself was a canon of Cologne. Even when the dignity was not, as it was in such cases, altogether honorary, it was sometimes combined with other offices which rendered the proper performance of its duties impossible ; and at first temporarily, but from the twelfth century permanently, canons were allowed to employ substitutes, "vicarii," for the discharge of their strictly clerical functions. So general did this employment of substitutes ultimately become, that the "vicars" of a cathedral chapter came themselves to be constituted into a corporation and to enjoy revenues of their own.

It was in this way that the retention by the canonical clergy of the right to hold private property came to subvert the original purpose for which they were established. The failure was unquestioned. Ivo, Bishop of Chartres, writing in the eleventh century, states the fact, and assigns as its cause " the coldness of the charity which would have all things common, and the reign of the cupidity which seeks not the things which are God's and one's neighbour's, but only those things which are one's own."[1] And in similar language a few years later Pope

[1] Ivon. Carnot., *Epist.*, 213, ed. Juret., p. 371.

## 182 GROWTH OF CHURCH INSTITUTIONS.

Urban II. says of the canonical life that "through the cooling of the zeal of the faithful it has almost wholly passed away."[1] The cause of the failure was so well understood, that the great movement which was made in the eleventh and twelfth centuries for the revival and reform of the system turned wholly upon this one point. The distinction between monks and canons in respect of holding private property was abolished by the reforming party, and since a passage in St. Augustine could be quoted in favour of a perfect community of goods among clergy, the name of that great Father was prefixed to a set of rules which rested on the idea of such a community as its leading principle. Henceforward all canons, whether of the bishop's church or of other churches, were divided into two kinds: those who did and those who did not accept the principle of abandoning private property. The former were called Augustinian or "regular," the latter were distinguished as "secular" canons. From the former came, in the course of the twelfth century, those who

---

[1] Urban, II., *Epist. ad clericos quosdam regul.*, ap. Mansi, *Concilia*, vol. xx., 713.

followed an even stricter rule, and who, from the birthplace of their founder, Norbert of Premontré, were known as "Premonstratensian" canons. These two groups of "regular" canons were popularly distinguished, from the colour of their respective habits, the former as Black, the latter as White Canons.

II. The history of these developments of the canonical system would carry us far beyond the limits of these pages, and we pass from it to consider the internal organisation of the canons or "chapter" of the bishop's church.

1. It has been already mentioned that whereas in the original rule of Chrodegang the bishop's representative as head of the clergy-house was the archdeacon, in the rule of Aachen he is called by the more general designation of "præpositus" or provost. But the new name was probably not intended to do more than cover the fact that there were communities of clergy living together besides the community of clergy attached to the bishop's church, away from the immediate control of the bishop and the bishop's ordinary representative. In the community of cathedral clergy the archdeacon

and the provost were, as a rule, the same person. Where, as at Rheims, they were separate officers, the provost was charged with the administration of the revenues of the clergy-house and with the provision for the physical needs of the clergy ; the archdeacon was charged with the supervision of their ecclesiastical functions. But whether the office of provost was combined with or separate from that of archdeacon, a certain difficulty arose from the fact that when the clergy passed from the clergy-house into the church, another officer took the precedence in Divine service. This was the archpresbyter, or, as he came to be usually called, the " dean " —a term which was so widely in use for other and varied purposes, that the origin of its use in this particular way cannot be certainly ascertained. It was inevitable that between two officers, each of whom in turn presided over the other, there should be a certain amount of friction ; and it is consequently not surprising to find that one or other of the two sometimes ceased to exist, and that some chapters had a dean without a provost, and others a provost without a dean ; sometimes also the provost was archpresbyter, and not archdeacon, and the dean archdeacon rather than archpresbyter.[1] The difficulty was increased by the fact that the exercise of the archidiaconal functions of the provost, and, as time went on, the large increase in the capitular funds which he had to administer, caused that officer to be so frequently absent from the church, as sometimes to lose his right of voting in the chapter. The dean, on the contrary, was not called away by any such extraneous duties, and it is consequently not surprising to find that in a large number of chapters he came to be the more important officer. There was probably the further circumstance in favour of the same tendency that whereas the provost, as archdeacon, was appointed by the bishop, and was regarded as being especially the bishop's officer, the dean was elected by the chapter, and being so elected, was more likely to guard the rights of the chapter against the bishop.[2] The older relation of the wo officers survives in our

---

[1] Instances will be found mentioned by Hinschius (*Das Kirchenrecht der Katholiken und Protestanten in Deutschland*, Bd. ii., p. 93).

[2] An instance of such election is that of Paris (Guérard, *ut supra*, p. c.).

own country, not in cathedrals, but in the colleges of Oxford, where the head of the society is called by the name of provost or by some equivalent designation, and in the older foundations is charged with especial duties in relation to their funds, while the dean occupies a lower place, but is charged with especial duties in relation to discipline and Divine worship.

After the provost or dean came the officer who, under the name "primicerius," had been mentioned in earlier times as the director of the lower grades of clerks, the subdeacons, acolyths, and readers, but who afterwards was more generally entitled "cantor" or "præcentor." At Cologne he had also the title "chori-episcopus," or superintendent of the choir, a title which must be carefully distinguished from that of chorepiscopus, or country bishop, of which mention has been made in a previous chapter.

After the precentor came the "scholasticus," or schoolmaster, who was charged with the instruction of the younger clerks, and who, from his also acting as the ordinary secretary of the whole body, was sometimes also entitled "cancellarius," or chancellor. When the instruction of other persons was added to that of the young clerks of the clergy-house, and the cathedral schools became important centres of learning, the scholasticus had the right to nominate his assistants, who bore the title of "rector scholarum" or "magister scholarum." Members of the University of Oxford will recognise a survival of this usage in the practice, which has only recently ceased to exist, of the annual appointment of the "Masters of the Schools" by the Chancellor's deputy.

Besides these there was a varying number of other officers, especially the "custos," or warden, whose office is not easy to distinguish from that of the "sacrista," or sacristan, and was no doubt frequently combined with it, and also with that of "thesaurarius," or treasurer,[1] and who had the care of the sacred vessels and lights and furniture.

Some or all of these officers, the number and the particular officers varying widely in different parts of Christendom, were distinguished as "prelates" or "dignitaries," and also by a

---

[1] The two offices of "custos" and "sacrista" are distinguished in the Canon Law ("X. de Off Sacr.," i., 26, 27).

word which had the same meaning as the fore-going, but which in France and England was more commonly applied to the holders of parochial benefices, that of " personæ," or parsons. The other canons were originally distinguished, according as they were in major or minor orders, into senior and junior canons ; afterwards came the distinction into canons capitular and canons non-capitular, according as they had or had not a voice in the chapter, the latter being also known as " domicelli." In time a further distinction followed. In the first instance each canon had his " præbenda," his proper share in the meat, drink, and clothing which were assigned to the clergy from the common church funds; when this was commuted for a money payment, it was still called by the same name ; but when, instead of the payment of a share of money from a common fund, lands or tithes were assigned to particular canons for their support, the term " præbenda " was transferred to the lands or tithes. And since there were some canons to whom lands or tithes were not so assigned, but who had no more than the ancient right to live in the common house and dine at the common table, a distinction grew up between those who were canons simply and those who were also "præbendarii," *i.e.*, who had an estate which yielded an income.

If we compare the original theory and practice of the canonical life with its final developments, the transformation will appear strange and almost incredible. The theory was that the clergy should live together, away from the risk of contamination by a corrupt society, in the perfect fraternity of a common dining-hall and a common sleeping-chamber; they came in practice to live in separate houses, within the cathedral precincts, but yet detached from each other, and to dine together only on great festivals. The theory was that they should take their several places in Divine service not only every day, but many times a day; they came in practice to be able to perform their duties in the choir in some cases entirely by deputy, and in almost all cases for limited periods and on fixed occasions. The theory was that they were officers of the whole community of which the bishop was the head, appointed freely by the community and by its head; they came in practice to be a close corporation, whose members were usually elected by co-optation, and who were in many cases not necessarily officers of the community—*i.e.*, in holy orders—at all. The theory was that out of the common offerings a common table was provided; they came in practice to have large separate revenues, each canon having the full rights of a tenant in fee over the lands annexed to his canonry. But the fact that the transformation has been great does not prove that it has been without benefit. Each development of the original principle has, on the contrary, borne splendid fruit. It has passed, like all human institutions, through its periods of overgrowth and decay. It has constantly needed, and it needs now, readaptation to new wants. But we cannot hesitate to thank God for the birth and growth of an institution which gave to our forefathers, and has continued to ourselves, not only the buildings and the chapters of our cathedrals, but also the colleges of our universities and the organisation of the universities themselves.

*THE CHAPTER AND THE DIOCESE.*

## XI.

### THE CHAPTER AND THE DIOCESE.

ONE of the most important of the constitutional changes which have taken place in the history of the Western Churches is that by which the clergy of the bishop's church, organised in the manner which has been described in the two preceding chapters, gradually took the place and absorbed the functions of the whole body of the clergy of the diocese. In earlier times there had been no other clergy than those of the bishop's church. As long as each city or rural district had its complete organisation, the bishop and all the clergy met day after day, or week after week, for the purposes of discipline and administration no less than of worship. In all these respects it is probable that the community originally acted as a whole, and that the sharp line of distinction which came to be rawn in later times between the officers of the community and its ordinary members did not exist. It would be interesting, but it would at the same time involve a longer statement than is here possible, to show by what slow steps the non-official part of the Christian communities came to lose in practice its original share in the administration of their affairs. It would be no less interesting, but it would be no less outside our present limits, to show the steps by which certain important functions which once belonged to the whole community, and afterwards passed into the exclusive hands of the clergy, were monopolised by the bishop. The purpose of the present chapter is to show in outline how certain parts of ecclesiastical administration not only ceased to be functions of the whole community, but became the special functions of the cathedral chapter.

The first distinction that arose among the clergy was a necessary result of the system of not giving to every community a complete organisation. It was inevitable that the detachment of presbyters from the church of a city, and their settlement with a quasi-independent position in small towns and rural districts, should produce in course of time a distinction between city and rural clergy. It was no less inevitable that those who remained at or near the bishop's church should meet together more frequently, and be more frequently consulted on questions of administration, than those who lived at some distance from the city. But the main cause of the distinction which afterwards arose was not local separation, but the growth of the system of separate endowments. So long as country presbyters were, like city presbyters, dependent for their maintenance upon the portion of the offerings which was assigned to them by the bishop, they were compelled to make periodical visits to the bishop's church. But when country churches began to have funds of their own, country presbyters began to resort so infrequently to the city, that legislation on the subject became necessary. It was found expedient that they should not only meet the bishop and the other clergy in council, but that they should do so at fixed times. Hence a distinction arose between he presbytery or ordinary council of the Church, which continued to meet week by week, and the larger council ["generalis synodus," "magna synodus"), which met only once or twice a year. The distinction is similar to that which has existed in the constitutional history of our own country between the Privy Council, which is in theory always near the person of the Sovereign, and the Great Council, or Parliament, which is summoned only from time to time. And in the one case no less than in the other a certain section of the smaller body, the cathedral chapter and the "cabinet" respectively, has come to exercise a considerable proportion of the functions which originally belonged to the larger body.

The final assignment of separate functions to the two bodies was not accomplished until far on in the Middle Ages. For many centuries the larger body consisted of the same members and had the same wide range of duties as before. It did not cease to be in theory, and to no small extent in practice also, what the first organised assemblies of Christians had been. In regard to its members, existing records specify not only presbyters, but deacons and subdeacons, and not only clergy, but laity : whether all members stood on the same footing and had an equal right of voting is uncertain ; but the existence of a variety of elements in the synod is beyond question.[1]

In regard to its functions, the records give instances of all kinds of administrative and many kinds of judicial acts : the creation of parishes and monasteries ; the recognition and confirmation of endowments ; the decision of controversies as to tithes ; and processes against heretics.[2]

The name "diocesan synod," by which the institution is known in its revived form in modern times, is first found in the thirteenth century : but in that century the institution

---

[1] The following are a few of many instances. At Como in 1010, " all the clerks and laity of the diocese " are specified (Mansi, vol. xix., 315) ; at Besançon in 1041, provosts, deans, cantors, archdeacons, succentors, abbots, archpresbyters, chaplains, deacons, and subdeacons (Mansi, vol. xix., 597) at Constance in 1094, the clergy with the dukes and other chief men of Germany (Mansi, vol. xx., 795) ; at Bamberg in 1087, " the whole number of those who were present at the synod, that is, the clergy (who were present) as a part of their holy obedience, the judges and other laymen bound by their oaths " (Hartzheim, *Concilia Germaniæ*, vol. iii., 206).

[2] Instances of each of these will be found collected by Hinschius, *Das Kirchenrecht*, Bd. iii., p. 587.

itself also ceased for the most part to exist: so far as it existed, its members were no longer the whole body of clergy and laity, but only the dignitaries of a diocese with the rectors of parishes; and its functions were narrowed partly by the growing interference of the papal see in the internal affairs of dioceses, partly by the growing concentration of power in the hands of the bishops, partly by the development of the functions of the smaller council which consisted of the cathedral chapter.

Those functions arose in the first instance naturally and out of the necessities of the case. There were many kinds of administrative acts which were still regarded as being the acts of the whole Church, but which could not wait for the periodical assemblies. The clergy and laity of the bishop's city and its neighbourhood were taken to represent the whole Church, and their consent was sufficient to give validity to what was done. It is difficult for those who are conversant only with the ecclesiastical usages of later times to realise how hard the original theory died. A long succession of documents might be quoted to show that until

## THE CHAPTER AND THE DIOCESE. 199

at least the middle of the twelfth century the concurrence of clergy and laity in the more important administrative acts of a diocese was ordinarily required. The change came through the influence of the popes. The victory of the ecclesiastical theory in the Concordat of Worms caused a gradual disregard of the laity; and the determination of the popes to make the cathedral chapters a check upon the tendencies to independence on the part of the bishops caused the disregard of any other clergy but those of the cathedral. The proofs of this are to be found in the additions to the earlier regulations of the Canon Law. One of the earliest of such proofs is a letter of Alexander III., in which he strongly reproves a bishop for frequently consulting the clergy and laity of his neighbourhood instead of the canons of his cathedral.[1] A series of subsequent decretals defines exactly the points in which a bishop could only act with the consent, or with the advice, of his chapter; and to the present day, in the view of the Canon Law, and subject only to the

---

[1] c. 5, X. de his quæ fiunt a prælato sine consensu capituli (iii. 10).

right, which remains in a bishop's discretion, of summoning the larger synod of his clergy, the corporate body of the chapter, and not either the clergy of the diocese as a whole or the clergy of the bishop's city, constitute the standing council of the diocese.

In many respects it might have been wished that in the working constitution of our own Church the powers of the chapter as a check upon bishops had been retained. Our own system is that of the later Middle Ages, in which the popes, abandoning their earlier support of the chapters against the bishops, gave facilities to the bishops to enable them to dispense with the consent of chapters. The dispensation has in many respects become not occasional but perpetual. The bishops have become possessed of an undesigned autocracy. The cathedral chapters exist as practically independent corporations, their diocesan functions, save in one important respect, having practically ceased. That respect is the election of bishops. It was the last function to pass into their hands, and it has remained in form till now. The primitive theory lingered on until a comparatively late period of the Middle Ages. The appointment of all officers had originally been in the hands of the community, but in the appointment of presbyters and deacons the share of the laity had been narrowed down to the simple right of approval, and the share of the clergy to that of bearing testimony, long before the canonical system began. The appointment of bishops, on the contrary, was never surrendered by the communities which had originally possessed it. The share of both laity and clergy in it was continually recognised and reasserted.[1] The reason for so continually reasserting a recognised rule was that the growing importance of bishops in the national economy had led to attempts on the part of kings to control or supersede their election by the Churches. The

---

[1] For example, in the sixth and seventh centuries, by the first Council of Clermont, in 535 (I. Conc. Arvern., c. 5); by the third Council of Orleans, in 538 (III. Conc. Aurel., c. 3); by the fourth Council of Orleans, in 541 (IV. Conc. Aurel., c. 5); by the fifth Council of Orleans, in 549 (V. Conc. Aurel., c. 10); by the third Council of Paris, in 557 (III. Conc. Paris, c. 8); by the second Council of Tours, in 567 (II. Conc. Turon., c. 9); by the fifth Council of Paris, in 615 (V. Conc. Paris, c. 1); by the Council of Reims, in 625 or 630 (Conc. Rem., c. 25); and by the Council of Chalons, in 649 or 664 (Conc. Cabil., c. 10).

interference of the kings took several forms. Sometimes a particular person was recommended for election; sometimes an election by the clergy and laity was set aside in favour of the king's nominee; probably in all cases the king's consent to an election was required. It is easy to see that in so important a matter the right of approval gradually drifted into the right of nomination. It is uncertain to what extent the form of election by clergy and people was preserved in the eighth century, but it is certain that, for a time at least, bishops were in fact appointed by the sovereign. Then came a reaction. The prevalence of simony caused a revival of the stricter practice of election. In a capitulary of 818 or 819 Lewis the Pious assented to the request of the clergy that bishops should be elected as of old, by the clergy and people, without money or favour.[1] For three centuries afterwards there was a constant struggle between Church and State on the subject, the former constantly reasserting its claim, the latter not denying the justice of

---

[1] Capit. Aquisgran., c. 2, ed. Pertz, i., p. 206; Capit. Ecclesiast., ed. Boret., p. 276.

the claim but simply setting it aside. Sometimes the claim was asked or conceded as a special privilege: for example, at the third Council of Valence, in 885, the king is to be asked to allow canonical election by the clergy and people, but if he insists on sending a nominee of his own, the nominee is to be respectfully examined as to his character and knowledge.[1] Sometimes it was reasserted in the decree of a council; for example, at Rome in 853, at Reims in 1049,[2] at Rome again in 1080. The struggle at length came to play an important part in civil as well as in ecclesiastical history, and resulted in the compromise known as the Concordat of Worms in 1122. The terms of the compromise were that the Emperor should allow the free election of bishops and their investiture as spiritual officers by the Church; that the Church should allow the elections to take place in the Emperor's presence; and the investiture of bishops

---

[1] III. Conc. Valent., c. 7, "sed etsi a servitio pii principis nostri aliquis clericorum venerit ut alicui civitati præponatur episcopus, timore casto sollicite examinetur primum cujus vitæ sit, deinde cujus scientiæ. . . ."

[2] An important council, at which Leo IX. presided.

as temporal officers by the State. But it is important to note that up to this period, wherever the election of bishops is mentioned, it is an election by the clergy and people of the diocese. The process of narrowing the electoral body was very slow. It can be traced as a natural development through several centuries. An assembly of all the clergy and all the people of a large diocese being practically impossible, the election, though open to all, came in fact to fall into the hands of those who were most interested in it,—the clergy of the city and the most influential among the laity. Hence in records of elections we find mention of, *e.g.*, the magnates and all the clergy,[1] and the count, the viscount, the nobles, and vassals, and all the people, the clergy moreover, the dean, the provost, the archdeacon, and all the clerks.[2] But after the Concordat of Worms we begin to find that the laity were excluded from a share in the actual election, their assent only being required. And since there was at the

---

[1] At Cologne in 933, *Vita Brunon.*, c. 11, ap. Pertz, *Scriptores*, vol. iv., p. 258.

At Bourges in 1052, Mansi, *Concilia*, vol. xix., 805.

same time a strong support of the cathedral chapters by the papal see, it is natural to find that election by the clergy only came to mean election by the canons only. Three stages are clearly marked in the Canon Law of the twelfth century. In the first of them the canons could not act alone, but only with the monks of the city or diocese; this stage is marked by a decree of the second Lateran Council in 1139, under Innocent II., which declares that if the monks, *religiosi viri*, be excluded by the canons from the election, the election will be null and void.[1] In the second stage it was ruled that the opposition of the monks should not override the votes of the canons, unless the former alleged a valid canonical objection to the election or the person elected; this stage is indicated by a letter of Alexander III. in 1169 to the chapter of Bremen. "Although in the election of a bishop the approval and assent of the sovereign ought to be required, laymen ought not to be admitted to the election. The election is to be made by the canons of the cathedral church and

---

[1] II. Conc. Lateran., c. 25, ap. Mansi, vol. xxi., 533.

the religious men who are in the city or diocese. At the same time, we do not say that the opposition of the religious men ought to outweigh the votes of the canons unless it should happen that a clear and canonical impediment stands in the way of either the election or the person elected."[1] In the final stage the chapter alone had the right of election, without being required to take the counsel of either monks or secular laity; this stage is marked by the decrees of Innocent III. and Gregory IX., which were incorporated into the body of Canon Law and formed the governing enactments on the subject for the future.[2]

By the end of the thirteenth century the election of bishops by cathedral chapters had become the common rule of the Western

---

[1] Alexand. III., *Ep. ad Capit. Brem., ap. Lappenberg, Hamburg. Urkundenbuch*, vol. i., p. 216, quoted by Hinschius, *Kirchenrecht*, Bd. ii., p. 603.

[2] c. 3, X., de caus. poss., ii., 12, "secundum statuta canonica electiones episcoporum ad cathedralium ecclesiarum clericos regulariter pertinere noscantur;" c. 56 (Greg. IX.), de Elect., i., 6, "Edicto perpetuo prohibemus ne per laicos cum canonicis pontificis electio præsumatur. Quæ si forte præsumpta fuerit, nullam obtineat formitatem, non obstante contraria consuetudine quæ dici debet potius corruptela."

Churches. The practice of our own country in this respect has been too clearly stated by Bishop Stubbs to need restatement in other words : " The struggle between Henry I. and Anselm on the question of investiture terminated in a compromise which placed the election in the hands of the chapters of the cathedrals, the consecration in that of the metropolitan and comprovincial bishops, and the bestowal of temporal estates and authority in the hands of the king. Stephen at his accession confirmed to the Churches the right of canonical election ; Henry II. and Richard observed the form ; and John, shortly before he granted the Great Charter, issued as a bribe to the bishops a shorter charter confirming the right of free election, subject to the royal licence and approval, neither of which was to be withheld without just cause. . . . The earlier practice, recorded in the Constitutions of Clarendon, according to which the election was made in the Curia Regis, in a national council, or in the royal chapel before the justiciary—a relic, perhaps, of the custom of nominating the prelates in the Witenagemot—was superseded by this enactment. The election took place in the chapter-house of the cathedral, and the king's wishes were signified by letter or message, not, as before, by direct dictation."[1] The history of the struggles which ensued, with varying fortunes, between the clergy, the papacy, and the Crown, falls beyond the limits of these pages. In every such struggle there was gain as well as loss; and the lesson which they collectively tell is the common lesson of all ecclesiastical history, that no system of Church government, and no machinery for working ecclesiastical institutions, is in itself perfect, but is constantly impaired by the forces of human nature that act upon it. And when so impaired, no legislation is strong enough to bring it back to its original state. Church government by cathedral chapters belongs already to the remote past; but it is for us and for our successors to solve the as yet unsolved problem how to replace it by a machinery which will be more efficient for the present and the future.

---

[1] Bishop Stubbs, *Constitutional History of England*, vol. iii., p. 295.

*THE CHANCEL.*

## XII.

### *THE CHANCEL.*

IT is natural to find that the multiplication of clergy-houses, and the consequently increased separation of the clergy from the laity in common life, had a tendency to accentuate the difference between clergy and laity in purely ecclesiastical respects. There are many indications that until the ninth century the line was by no means so sharply drawn as in the Middle Ages and in modern times. The Council of Reims, for example, early in the seventh century enacted that no layman is to be constituted archpresbyter without being ordained clerk.[1] An edict of Charles the Great in 805 enacted, in a similar way, that archdeacons should not be laymen.[2]

---

[1] Conc. Remens., A. D. 625 (630), c. 19.
[2] Capit. duplex ad Theodon. Vill., c. 15, ap. Pertz, M. G. H., i., 132, and Boretius, p. 122.

A Bishop of Bourges in 850 issued an order to his clergy that a layman should not read the Epistle.[1] It was an indication of the same tendency that stress came again to be laid, and in most countries has continued to be laid ever since, on the use of a distinctive dress by the clergy in ordinary life. Partly through tradition and partly by rule, the clergy had generally continued to wear the long hooded robe (casula) of the Roman provincials, in contrast to the short cloak (sagum) of the Teutons and Celts. In the capitulary which Carlman put forth at the instance of Boniface in 742, and again in the capitulary of his brother Pippin in 744, it was enacted that clerks should not wear lay dress.[2] The rule became invariable that the distinctive dress should always be worn, and that clerks should not go out of doors without it.[3]

---

[1] Capit. Rodolf. Bituric., c. 10, ap. Mansi, xiv., 948.

[2] Karlmanni principis capitulare, c. 7, Pippini principis capitulare Suessionense, c. 3, ap. Pertz, M. G. H., *Legum*, vol. i., pp. 16, 21 ; Boretius, pp. 26, 29.

[3] Conc. Mogunt., A.D. 813, c. 28 ; Conc. Rom., A.D. 853, c. 12.

## THE CHANCEL.

But the main differences between clergy and laity were those which expressed themselves in relation to Divine service. In the first place, a greater emphasis than before came to be given to the idea of the sanctity of the material church and of the material altar. Charles the Great included in the first capitulary which he issued a regulation that no priest should presume to celebrate mass except in places dedicated to God, or on tables which a bishop had consecrated.[1] The rule was repeated at Aachen in 801 (802), in regulations which are sometimes ascribed to the Emperor and sometimes to the bishops,[2] and having been incorporated in the pseudo-Isidorian decretals, it became so universal in its operation that even to the present day, and in Reformed communions, the celebration of the Eucharist in places other than those which have been specially dedicated to the service of God is commonly regarded with disfavour.[3]

---

[1] Karoli M. Capitulare Generale, A.D. 769—771, c. 14, Pertz, vol. i., p. 34.

[2] Capit. Aquisgran., c. 9, Pertz, vol. i., p. 87; Boretius, p. 106.

[3] The regulations of the ninth century, which governed

This growing idea of the special sanctity of the church and the altar led to a series of regulations which had the effect of separating the laity from the clergy in church by material barriers which had been unknown in early times. There had always been a special seat for the Church officers; there had also frequently been low railings for obvious purposes of order. But the communion table had been between the place of the clergy and that of the people, and the people had had free access to it. A local Eastern council of the fourth century, in a series of regulations for the better order of service, forbade the laity to go to

---

subsequent practice, are important enough to be specially noted: they are, mainly, the Council of Chalons in 813, c. 49, in Mansi, xiv., 104; the capitularies of Lewis the Pious and Lothair in 829, c. 12, ap. Pertz, *Legum*, vol. i., p. 342, and in the Council of Paris of the same year, c. 47, and lib. iii., c. 6; the capitularies of Lewis the German in 851, c. 24, in Pertz, vol. i., p. 415; the capitularies of Lewis II. in 856, c. 14, in Pertz, vol. i., p. 440; the capitularies of Charles II. in 876, c. 3, Pertz, vol. i., p. 531; the Council of Metz in 888, c. 8, in Mansi, xviii., 80; the regulations of Bishop Theodulf of Orleans, c. 11, in Mansi, xiii., 997, and of Bishop Rudolf of Bourges, in Mansi, xiv., 946. The passages of the pseudo-Isidorian decretals are *Ex Synod. gestis Silvestr.*, c. 9; Hinschius, p. 453; *Decret. Felicis IV.*, *ibid.*, p. 698.

THE CHANCEL. 215

the altar to communicate;[1] but although this regulation was revived, with many other such regulations, in later times, there is no evidence that it marked a general custom in either East or West. A Gallican council in the middle of the sixth century requires, as a matter of order, that during the service the people should be separate from the choir and clergy, but it adds the express reservation that "for purposes of praying and communicating the Holy of Holies, as the custom is, should be open to both laymen and women."[2] The paintings in some of the earliest missals which have come down to us represent the people on one side of the communion table and the priest on the other, with no barrier between them, and obviously about to communicate where they stand.[3] Two changes were gradually brought about: the one excluded laymen from access to the altar, the other from access to the choir. The former was probably the result, mainly,

---

[1] Conc. Laod., c. 19.
[2] II. Conc. Turon., A.D. 567, c. 4.
[3] For example, in the Metz Sacramentary in the National Library at Paris, No. 9428, probably of the ninth century.

of a change in the conception of the nature of the Eucharist ; the growth of the ideas which ultimately expressed themselves in the theory of Transubstantiation diffused a feeling of awe in reference to the consecrated elements which made unconsecrated persons reluctant to approach them. But the latter was the direct result of the canonical system, and came about rather by the slow force of circumstances than by the action of ideas upon practice. For the establishment of clergy-houses in the immediate vicinity of bishops' churches, and the requirement that those who lived in them, both young and old, should attend Divine service several times every day, naturally caused a large proportion of the services of such churches to be attended by clergy only. There were two immediate effects which soon came to be marked in the structure of the buildings.

1. The clergy of a church were more numerous, and required a larger space. The apse was no longer able to contain the presbyters. The accustomed space between the apse and the nave was no longer able to contain the lower orders of clerks. It became necessary to place

the apse at a farther distance from the nave, by elongating its side walls. In this way what is now known as the choir, or chancel, was formed. It was a mode of providing room for the increased numbers of the clergy.[1] And when it had been thus formed two other modifications of the structural arrangement became desirable. The diocesan arrangement gradually yielded to the arrangement of the clergy-house: the bishop was so frequently absent that the head of the clergy in the clergy-house became the virtual head of the clergy in the church. But since he could not sit in the bishop's seat, and since, in the absence of the bishop, the apse came to be deserted, a place of honour was found for him at the entrance to the elongated choir ; and since also it was necessary to have due order, and to give fixed places to the several members of the capitular

---

[1] It may be noted that Paul Warnefrid, in giving an account of Chrodegang of Metz, who first formulated a canonical rule, mentions that he not only introduced into his church the Roman order and the Roman plain-song, but also constructed a presbytery in the two churches of Metz (Paul Warnefrid, *Gesta Episc. Mettens*, ap. Pertz, *Scriptorum*, vol. ii., p. 268).

body, rows of seats, each seat being assigned to a definite person, were arranged along the walls, as in the chapel of a monastery. This is the origin of what are now known as "stalls."[1]

2. The second effect was that the part of the church which was thus almost exclusively used by the clergy, and in which services were performed several times a day, came to be separated from the rest of the church by a screen. It is possible that in the first instance the erection of such a screen was due to the prosaic reason of a desire to protect the clergy from the cold. The reason was, in any case, different from that which led to the erection of screens in Eastern churches, for the "iconostasis," or screen, in an Eastern church separates not the clergy from the laity, but the place of the altar, into which only the officiating priest and his assistants enter, from the ordinary place of the clergy and choir;

---

[1] Those who have time to study the history of the structural arrangement of churches will find ample materials in the elaborate and as yet unfinished work of Dekio and von Bezold, *Die Kirchliche Baukunst des Abenlandes*, Stuttgart, 1884.

it corresponds to the altar rails of Western churches, over which in the Middle Ages a curtain was sometimes suspended for the same purpose as that which the iconostasis was intended to serve, namely to protect the celebration of the " holy mysteries " from intruding eyes.

The effect of the introduction of screens had an influence which has left marked effects unto the present day upon the relations of the clergy both to the laity and to the bishop.

(1) The altar appears to have remained in its usual position, on the line of division between the place of the clergy and that of the laity. When this line of division was marked by a screen, the altar remained just outside it; the laity came up to this altar to make their offerings and to communicate, and it was known way of distinction as the altar of the laity. But since the existence of a screen made the position of this altar inconvenient to the clergy, another altar was placed, in ordinary parish churches against the wall at the end of the chancel, and in an apsidal bishop's

church on the chord of the apse; in either case the communion of the clergy came to be distinct from the communion of the laity, and the distinction was further emphasised by the growth, in a new form, of the idea of the Eucharist as a sacrifice. In course of time chancels came to be very general in both cathedral and parish churches; and in course of time also the altar of the laity at the entrance of the chancel lost its importance, and ceased to exist. But the collegiate type, with its long chancel, which grew out of the necessities of the canonical life, has left a mark upon the structure of churches which even we in modern times are only just beginning to disregard. The continued erection of long chancels in parish churches is a remarkable instance of the tenacity with which ancient types survive, in spite of the disappearance of the causes out of which they grew.

(2) In many districts of the West and North it became the practice to construct a passage round the choir, partly for processions, and partly to serve as a base upon which chapels and chantries might be built. Where this was

done, it became necessary to protect the clergy from the cold by constructing wooden screens, or in some cases stone walls, along the sides of the choir between it and the passage round it. Hence the place of the clergy was separated even more conspicuously than before from the place of the laity. It was a sort of church within the church, enclosed by walls, entered only by gates, which were commonly shut, and ordinarily accessible only to those who wore a special dress.[1]

For there is another result of the canonical life which has been no less permanent than the structural arrangements of churches. The climate of the North was not less severe in the Middle Ages than it is now, and at the same time artificial modes of producing heat were both fewer and more cumbrous. The cold was warded off not so much by fires as

---

[1] The best typical example of this "church within the church" which is known to the writer is that of the Cathedral of Albi, where there are not, as commonly elsewhere, any pillars to mark a structural division, but the greater and the smaller church are under a single unbroken roof. The service for the people is held at the western end, the altar being placed under the arch of the tower.

by the use of warmer clothing than is now commonly worn. Furs were in ordinary use, and the ordinary winter dress of those who lived the canonical life was a fur coat. Such a coat was allowed also to monks, and is prescribed in the statutes of several orders. But between canons and monks there was a point of difference which seems to have been universally maintained. A monk might not wear linen; a canon might do so. A monk must appear, whether in a church or in a monastery, in his woollen cowl; a canon threw a linen blouse over his fur coat, and was thereby known to be a canon and not a monk. There is an anecdote in one of the histories of St. Gall which will illustrate this point. Solomon, afterwards Bishop of Constance and Abbot of St. Gall, used in earlier days to go to the monastery, to the annoyance of the monks, without being himself a monk; it was part of the annoyance that in doing so he wore, as he was entitled to do, a canon's linen dress; once, when he offered a monk a present of a fur coat, the monk in return offered him a cowl, as being a more proper dress to wear in a monastery.[1] Another instance of a similar kind is afforded by the fact that when there was a doubt whether the clergy at Cahors were monks or canons, the fact that they wore surplices was held to be proof conclusive that they were the latter.

The linen blouse which was thus worn by canons, as a distinctive mark of their order, over the fur coat, or "pelisse," was commonly known as the "overpelisse," "superpelliceum," or "surplice." It was not a clerical dress, since there were canons who were not clerks. It was a becoming mark of an ecclesiastical order. All who had a title to enter the choir, whether laymen or clerks, wore it to designate their status ; and it survived the changes of the Reformation because it was in the eyes of all but a small fraction of the Reformers too innocent to be worth abolishing.

The strength of the canonical system may be estimated not only by the general prevalence of the usages which have been described, but also,

---

[1] Ekkehardi IV., *Casus S. Galli*, in Pertz, M. G. H., *Scriptorum*, vol. ii., p. 79. The point of the objection is tersely expressed in the phrase "lineus diatim adiit."

and even more significantly, by the change in the position of the bishop's seat in his own church. In early times there could have been no doubt in the mind of any one who entered a bishop's church that the bishop was its president. Where the ancient seat remains, as at Torcello or Grado, it is raised high in the centre of the apse; and even where the ancient seat has been replaced by a later one it is still in an obvious place of authority. But gradually in most parts of Northern Christendom the apse came to be disused. The presbysters sat not round their bishop, but, as I have mentioned above, in their assigned places in the choir. The Eucharist was celebrated by one who stood not, as in early times, behind the altar, but in front of it. The bishop's seat, at first perhaps only temporarily and for convenience in the changed order of celebration, but at last permanently, was transferred from the apse to the choir. The bishop took his seat not as head of the whole body, but as a member of it. He was placed at the end of the row of canons. Sometimes, as in some English cathedrals to the present day, he was required, by a strange irony

## THE CHANCEL.

of circumstances, to be himself a canon. The diocese was merged in the chapter; and the original inmates of the bishop's house, who formed only a portion of the whole number of his clergy, and who were governed in his absence by his deputy, came to affect to recognise his existence only so far as he became one of their number, and sat with them in their row of stalls.

The sketch which has been given in these pages of the growth of some Church institutions is necessarily incomplete. But even from an incomplete sketch, two points come clearly to light. The one is that many institutions and elements of institutions which have sometimes been thought to belong to primitive Christianity belong, in fact, to the Middle Ages. In the minds of many persons, no doubt, the past centuries of Christianity seem to be all alike shrouded in a common mist, and the institutions of one age are not distinguishable from those of another; but it is impossible to look without regret at the reckless statements which are frequently made in reference to practices which, however great their practical value, and however great the sanction which long usage has given them, still rest upon proved utility and not upon a positive Divine command. The other point is that ecclesiastical institutions have shown a remarkable power of adapting themselves in successive ages to the new needs of men. They were not made of iron, designed to crush into a single unvarying form the innumerable types of human character or the shifting phenomena of Christian history. They were gifted with a vitality which, preserving always the same Divine principle of life, was at the same time continually adapting their forms to meet the new conditions of society. Nor can we believe that the form under which we ourselves live is final. The wisdom of our forefathers must yield to the wisdom of our contemporaries, and the wisdom of our contemporaries will in its turn yield to the wisdom of our children. And yet it is possible even for one who accepts this inevitable law of change to look with regret at some of the ancient forms which are passing into the world of shadows, and to express the hope that from the mists of the unrealised future there may come forth institutions as fruitful for good to the souls of men as those of the beautiful but irrecoverable past.

www.ingramcontent.com/pod-product-compliance
Lightning Source LLC
Chambersburg PA
CBHW070311230426
43663CB00011B/2076